INVITATION TO GLOBALOGY:

INVITATION TO GLOBALOGY:

An Alien Perspective

Michael Cruit

and

Pat Lauderdale

SRI Press,
Social Research Institute of Arizona
Tempe, AZ

ISBN: 978-0-9978854-0-8

Copyright © 2016 SRI Press
First edition published 2014; Second edition 2016.

All rights reserved. This book or any portion thereof may not be reproduced or used in any manner whatsoever without the express written permission of the publisher except for the use of brief quotations in a book review.

Front cover illustration: NASA, Visible Earth. Image created by Reto Stockli with the help of Alan Nelson, under the leadership of Fritz Hasler; 180° rotation.

Back cover illustration: Back cover illustration: High-Energy X-ray View of "Hand of God," NASA/JPL-Caltech/McGill

Cover and book design by Kathryn Wilham

Contents

i

INTRODUCTION

We arrived safely at Earth's solar system and we are in orbit around Earth. It is one of the most beautiful planets we've ever seen. It is blue, white, green, and brown, with an oxygen-rich atmosphere and more water than land mass. It orbits a medium-sized sun at a perfect distance, allowing for a variable yet comfortable climate. These favorable conditions have led to an incredibly rich and diverse eco-system, including the human beings.

We were relieved to discover that use of atomic power as weapons did not continue after Earth's "second world war." Various countries, nonetheless, continue to develop and build nuclear weapons, and many thousands of atomic warheads are still deployed.

Our first responsibility was to learn more about every-day, "real" human behavior and discern patterns or clues that help us understand the human race and its relationship to Earth. Our initial investigations revealed that the social realities on Earth are far more complex than we had imagined. We knew the humans would be much different from us, but we never imagined they'd be so different from each other.

Furthermore, we discovered that Earth's atmospheric conditions are changing rapidly, exerting stress on the entire ecosphere. Although Earth offers ideal conditions for a great diversity of life-forms living harmoniously, we confirm that Earth is now experiencing a mass extinction event, apparently the sixth such event in its history.

We have examined human relationships in the new era of globalization. In one sense, instantaneous communications and satellite broadcasts have brought Earth's cultures closer together than ever. This closeness, which often appears to be superficial, has produced a double-edged impact; learning about strange cultures can either enlighten or threaten. In fact, there are several wars and armed conflicts now occurring in various places on Earth (Bacevich, 2015).

Globalization also has led to a greater awareness of the human relationship with Earth's ecosphere. Increasingly, the humans are compelled to perceive the Earth as their primal Mother. In the last few years the world's media have broadcast loud and conflicting reports about the condition of Earth's atmosphere and climate, setting off a cantankerous public debate that continues to rage. Conclusions and predictions by climate scientists and meteorologists are met by a cloud of controversy and confusion (McPherson, 2013; Sachs, 2015).

According to our preliminary investigations, Earth's atmosphere is changing. Since all eco-systems evolve according to the atmosphere, this produces great stress on the planetary ecosphere. Carbon levels in Earth's atmosphere and in the oceans have reached record densities—levels not seen in centuries—and this change is having an impact on global weather patterns, which in turn impacts heavily on plants and animals. During the current mass extinction event, over two hundred plant or animal species go extinct every day.

Initially, we chose to focus our investigations on sociological research. The human science of sociology observes and studies human behavior as it occurs within social and environmental contexts. It encompasses a range of study from whole societies to small groups of three or more people. It claims license to investigate significant environmental contexts supporting social interaction.

Yet, since most sociologists are subject to the same socialization process as other people, and influenced by the same cultural idiosyncrasies, their observations will likely be influenced by these particular perspectives (Berger, 2011). These perspectives often are cultural in nature and thus limit and obscure the possibilities; they act as inhibitors to other, alternative perspectives.

Most of Earth's sociologists regard social reality through the prism of their own peculiar cultural experience. This perception introduces a certain amount of bias and distortion, which is understandable. When these sociologists collaborate with others of the same culture, the biases and distortions are likely to remain undetected.

Sociologists also internalize the culture of academia. Prolonged exposure and participation inside academia creates high levels of conformity and predictability. Academics have been trained in specific ways, and their training impacts how they approach their studies and evaluate the outcomes. These cultural influences produce a particular mindset that tends to become "locked in," making it extremely difficult for them to step back and regard social reality from an entirely different perspective.

This "indoctrination process" is not specific to academia and sociologists. The "world view" within any specific culture emerges partly as a consequence of social organization. For example, institutions such as education and religion are infused with cultural ideals such as corporatism, consumerism, conformity and obedience, and the resulting social structure is "reality," from which most citizens derive social rules, values, and beliefs.

We reexamined the ideas of the Italian thinker named Antonio Gramsci, whose discussions about cultural domination and construction of reality led to the concept of "hegemony." Following Gramsci, Annamarie Oliverio (1998) has suggested that hegemony is an order in which a certain way of life and thought is dominant, in which one world view permeates customs and political and religious ideas, especially their intellectual and moral connotations. She stresses the importance of understanding the manipulation of culture as a form of domination, where various dominant groups with a coincidence of interests will impress these interests on citizens from the cradle onward, through the socialization process.

Hegemony is not simply a matter of applying political power, but a way of thinking. In fact, hegemony may be regarded as social coercion applied by the governors in an effort to gain the consent of the governed. Gramsci discusses this connection between hegemony and what he calls "the manufacture of consent." The shape of a culture and the social structure that supports it will usually reflect the values and interests of the dominate powers. One of our tasks in this report is to focus on the question of how human social reality is constructed and who are the constructors.

As a way to counter-balance the cultural bias from each country, the perspective of this report will focus upon a global level. A global perspective helps us move beyond the details, distractions, and passions of "national identities." We call this perspective "globalogy."

Globalogy acknowledges that the Earth's entire global community—flora and fauna, including humans—has moved into new and unknown territory. The best way to gauge or describe this new territory is from a global perspective. And, for us, globalogy will include careful attention to relations of power, the surrounding environmental context, and all Earth's ecosystems.

Many countries on Earth have become a "world power" at certain times in history. Since the 1400s the planet has seen the shift in power from Portugal to Spain to the Netherlands to France, to Great Britain, and now to the United States (Frank and Denemark, 2015; Leonard and Taylor, 2016). It's not too much to describe the U.S. as an "empire," at least in terms of global presence economically and militarily. For example, the U.S. maintains over eight hundred military bases around the world, far more than all other countries; in addition, its "aircraft carriers and submarines" roam the world, "projecting power."

Because of this domination and control, we'll initially concentrate our observations on the U.S., and then broaden our observations to the global level. Through the hegemonic process of cultural transmission, most technologically advanced cultures in the world today reflect various versions of the U.S. culture.

This process, however, is changing rapidly. We arrived at Earth at a propitious moment in its history. The geopolitical power arrangements that were forged during the last 100 years of armed conquest and domination are beginning to crumble. Although the United States still ranks first in economic and military power—its "empire" intact—other nations are rising fast and forming alliances designed to counter U.S. political and cultural domination. The balance of power is shifting to China, Russia, and Asia in general. Such challenges to U.S. domination include efforts by China, Japan, and Russia to eventually replace the U.S. dollar as the world's fixed currency (*The Japan Times*, May 24, 2014).

China is the largest purchaser of major U.S. treasury securities. According to the World Gold Council, China has been purchasing great quantities of gold—mainly in an effort to bolster confidence and value of its own currency, the renminbi. The Russian central bank has also been buying gold, expressing its disdain for the dollar. Moreover, Russia and China concluded a major economic alliance; for the next 30 years Russia probably will supply China with natural gas. The contract is worth $400 billion, which is greater than the gross domestic product of South Africa. This is a very lucrative arrangement for both countries, but also significant politically; by turning toward each other, Russia and China partly turn their backs on the United States and Europe.

Many of the conversations we have heard so-far in old academic circles focus upon political economy, and it's true that political power and money appear to be very important. However, we'll also report other voices from different perspectives and concerns, many of whom are considered political deviants because they challenge the status quo for a higher moral good (Lauderdale, 2011). Now, we turn to controversies over what humans call "consumerism."

CHAPTER 1: CONSUMERISM

One of the most common activities among humans on Earth is consumption. The majority of Earth's people live in urban centers where a consumer lifestyle seems necessary, and not just for food. Very few humans make their own shoes, clothes, furniture, dishes, house, electricity, or means of transportation. In fact, most don't know how to repair these new essentials, such as automobiles and computers. Most of these "necessities of life" are manufactured and sold to humans by corporate entities—but only if the humans have the means to purchase these things, which usually means "money" (paper currency or coins with a specific symbolic value, or something called "credit"). Usually, humans earn money from "work" or "inheritance" or "criminal activities."

We discovered significant dependency on corporate organizations: most corporations sell life to a great majority of humans. In general, most of Earth's people can buy a few of these necessities, even though a third of the planet lives on the equivalent of only a dollar or two a day.

The idea of consumption, however, goes far beyond these "necessities" to a glut of products and services designed for comfort, luxury, or prestige—so-called "consumer goods."

Consumption has penetrated to most facets of human experience and is connected intimately with personal identities.

Mass marketing and mass consumption appear to work together. "Mass marketing" is appealing to millions of people, encouraging them to "consume" various products and services.

Mass marketing in the United States had its infancy during the 1930s and '40s, the "golden age of radio." Nationally syndicated programs beamed signals directly into the homes of millions, delivering "entertainment" supported by commercials for "consumer products and services." However, the prolonged stagnation of the U.S. economic depression and the onset of a world war interrupted the new practice of mass consumption. On the other hand, the activity of warfare helped build factories and developed new manufacturing methods. These manufacturing assets formed the foundation of the next phase of mass marketing and mass consumption, including the nascent "defense" industry, which grew eventually into a giant military/industrial complex.

We discovered a book that gave us helpful insights: *A Consumers' Republic: The Politics of Mass Consumption in Postwar America* by Lisabeth Cohen (2003). She argues that mass consumption is based on the assumption that it is good for economic growth and consistent with democratic ideals. Cohen (2003) cites an article from a 1947 issue of *Harper's* magazine: "The rich man smokes the same sort of cigarettes as the poor man, shaves with the same sort of razor, uses the same sort of telephone, vacuum cleaner, radio and TV set, and drives a car with only minor variations" (p. 239).

It was thought that private consumption would result in public benefit. We traced this idea to an eighteenth century philosopher named Adam Smith. He argued that a society of individuals engaged in their own self-interest would result in the greatest good for all. Smith believed this to be a "natural" process—the inevitable outcome of a free-market economy. He was reported to have said this: "Don't try to do good. Let good emerge as the by-product of selfishness." Although Smith did not use the word "capitalism," he is widely regarded as the "founder" of this particular economic system (Heilbroner, 1999:9).

We need to stress, however, that these ideas were formulated over 200 years ago when Earth and countries like the United States were much different places. Today, in the United States and in much of the world, there is no such thing as a "free market." Governments routinely impose import and export taxes, enforce quotas and conditions on foreign goods, and regulate capital flow. Plus, giant multinational corporations have defeated the notion of "competition."

Nevertheless, this earlier version of "capitalism" is still attractive to numerous government administrators, mainly because it offers a semblance of social equality without redistribution of wealth. Top economists and government leaders have argued that economic growth from increased product development and mass purchasing power would raise the lifestyles of all segments of society, just as an incoming ocean tide lifts all boats big and small.

At first, the promise of mass consumption and equal distribution seemed fulfilled; intense postwar economic expansion in the United States and other countries lifted millions of people to unprecedented levels of consumption. Millions of returning U.S. soldiers benefitted from the GI Bill and low interest home loans (there were restrictions, however, regarding African-American veterans, mainly because of ethnic biases). By the 1950s a large percentage of the U.S. population owned their own homes, there was near-full employment, labor unions were healthy and active, and corporations continued to profit.

However, according to Cohen, by the late 1950s, marketers and corporations worried that the mass market might become saturated, resulting in a decrease in demand and sales. The solution, emerging in the early 1960s, was what Cohen calls "market segmentation"; that is, the break-down of the mass of consumers into constituent groupings according to age, education, gender, income, profession, and ethnicity—each segment to be sold different products, or the same products in different ways.

In the United States and other technologically advanced countries during the 1950s, there were only a few brands of deodorant available. Then, suddenly, there was deodorant for men and a different deodorant for women; then deodorant for teen girls and teen boys; then came sticks, liquids, roll-ons, and sprays in every imaginable odor. Shampoo is another example. In the early days of mass consumption, shampoo was a fairly standard product. Now there are types of shampoo for every possible hair color and condition; for all different ages; and for men, women, children, babies, and even domestic animals.

In this regard, we have identified an important contribution by Pierre Martineau in an article featured in the 1958 issue of the *Journal of Marketing*. He claimed consumers could also be separated by "social class." A person of a particular social position "is profoundly different in his mode of thinking and his way of handling the world.... Where he buys and what he buys will differ not only by economics but in *symbolic value*" (Martineau, 1958:122). We added the italics to stress the importance of the linkage between "consumer products" and their symbolic meaning. Consumption is not simply a matter of satisfying private interests and tastes, but it also announces one's social position in relation to other members of the society. For example, a Rolls Royce Silver Cloud floating by on the street will likely garner attention and admiration, and for the person who owns it, whereas all other vehicles usually remain anonymous, often almost invisible.

This market segmentation allowed for a whole range of new product possibilities, from "specialty stores" selling luxury items, to discount stores selling low-quality, low-priced goods. Further, market segmentation reinforced and exaggerated the divisions among various social groups. According to Cohen (2003), "Americans were propelled away from the common ground of the mass toward the divided, and often unequal, territories of population fragments, thereby accentuating everything that made them different from each other and undermining any broad-based political agenda designed to serve the public good" (p. 239).

By assigning symbols to "social class," the *quantity* and *quality* of "consumer goods" often become more valuable than the things themselves, mainly because they reflect directly on the owner. Most humans seem to define their personal identities in terms of those things preceded by the pronoun "my"—house, car, property, posture, parents, school, vocabulary, job, wife, and husband. These things announce *who they are*. They judge and are judged by the things they attach to their person, even if it's only the shirt on their back.

The encouragement of a consumer lifestyle is driven not only by the media, but also by various cultural outlets, including education and religion. Christmas, as only one example, is an important religious tradition among many humans and also the biggest shopping season, when huge amounts of goods and services are consumed, mostly in the more prosperous northern hemisphere.

Inside the consumerist Cultural Model, children learn early that the things they claim reflect on who they are. This cultural philosophy leads to a desire to accumulate more things and those of higher quality; for example, better grades or a nicer toy. Thus, early in life a pattern of consumption is established whereby one's personal identity grows or diminishes in proportion to what one owns or doesn't own (including awards, prizes, grades, and degrees). Typically, the more valuable things one owns, the more status or attention one commands. Status, power, and attention seem to be what most humans are taught to crave.

The reverse is also true; if the things are considered "bad" or unworthy, then these sentiments also reflect on their identity.

We observed "report card time" in a U.S. Catholic grade school. The teacher, dressed in the special clothes of a religious order, called the children up to her desk one by one, in alphabetical order, while the rest of the class watched and listened. By taking note of the teacher's and students' expressions, we perceived a great range of emotions—from delight to mortification. The "good" grades and "bad" grades reflected directly on the students, and we felt the joy, heat, and embarrassment.

There exists a powerful symbolic element to the things humans attach to themselves. In most cases, these possessions announce their level and status of consumption. For example, clothing bought from a second-hand store, and a handmade suit of the finest cashmere, perform the exact same function—covering the body with clothes. However, the *quality* of the clothes is symbolic and measures one's position in the great competitive game of consumption. Why would someone pay $5,000 for a suit if they only wanted to cover themselves? They don't; they pay for the *image*, which reflects on their identity. On the other hand, there may be those who buy clothes at second-hand stores because this is also an image. The same is true for most consumer goods and services. In any case, most humans are well aware of projecting a particular "look" through the arrangement and type of clothes and ornaments they place on or near their bodies, including the decoration of body parts—tattoos, piercings, etc. This *look* is the result of on-going social discourse with close friends, family, and associates.

In fact, humans used to regard employment categories in reference to clothes; there were "white collar" jobs and "blue collar" jobs. People working in buildings or "offices" usually wear name-brand or quality clothing, while people working in warehouses, factories, or retail outlets wear an entirely different set of clothes—sometimes corporate uniforms. There is still a definite status ranking in these two categories, although internet entrepreneurs make the differentiation more complex.

The significance and meaning of these differences are not clear to us. However, along with other parts of the division of labor, there is also this element of a visual-symbolic nature. Moreover, there are vast differences in income levels between these two categories; the humans wearing suits earn much more than those not wearing suits, and yet it is the "not suit" humans who produce, assemble, and sweat! Again, this behavior is confusing to us, yet it is generally true in most countries on Earth.

We watched an experiment conducted by university students in a large urban center in the U.S. Midwest. The students observed people's reactions by crossing city streets while wearing different sets of clothes and appearances. They crossed the street against red lights and observed the reactions of other pedestrians.

First, they sent out a student dressed as a wealthy business-person—fine suit and tie, nice haircut, leather briefcase, shiny shoes. We noted that several people stepped out behind the businessperson and followed him across the street against the red light. Then the students sent out someone dressed in soiled clothes, with a dirty face and bare feet. The reactions were dramatically different. Hardly anyone followed the "poor" person; in fact, they seemed to shrink from his presence. When he crossed the street against the red light, we witnessed expressions of disapproval.

This propensity to make snap judgments based on appearances has enriched many corporations making and selling "personal grooming" products and clothing. In fact, some "clothing lines" claim to be high fashion or "designer" clothes, often with the names of famous designers proudly displayed: Armani, Gucci, Ralph Lauren, Prada, Gloria Vanderbilt, Dior, and Calvin Klein. These clothes command the highest prices, not just because of quality—which might be marginal or imaginary—but even more for their *symbolic* value. They make a statement about a human's identity and values. Once again, we point out the importance humans place on *image*, and not just on the cultural, everyday level, but permeating the political realm, entertainment, schools, universities, and religions.

Apart from sheer survival, one of the most powerful motives for engaging in "work" is to earn the money to spend and consume. In general, it seems that the more money one makes, the higher the level of consumption. In wealthy societies it is usually true that the higher one's education level, the higher the level of income and consumption.

However, if one is disadvantaged because of poor education, broken home, or other domestic troubles, the motivation to accumulate and consume will likely remain unfulfilled or delayed. Even if someone has a job and the pay is minimum wage or average, the motive to consume will have to be curtailed and amended; one buys sub-quality products at discount prices, shops during "sales," and/or collects coupons.

These are the patient, hard-working millions of citizens who move within the boundaries of the formal law. Others are not so patient about satisfying their consumerist desires and resort to illicit activities. In fact, this constant emphasis on the accumulation of "consumer goods" is likely a major motive in most crimes against property—including "white collar" and corporate crime.

There are many levels and symbolic meanings in the process of consumption. Beatrice Kaufman, wife of playwright George S. Kaufman, once observed, "I've been rich and I've been poor, and rich is better." A higher level of consumption appears to enhance a human's identity, and also protects their identity, and even creates a new identity. Limousines, private aircraft, and walled, guarded "estates" protect the owners' identities by rendering them nearly invisible to public view, except under very controlled circumstances. Obvious examples of creating identities are illustrated by celebrities and politicians who purchase the services of public relations firms to project and maintain a particular image.

Most of Earth's population is often referred to as "consumers," but the consumer is not the only actor in the process of consumption; there are also the *sellers* and *makers* of "consumer products." In today's global reality, most of the products and services humans consume are made and sold by private corporations. These corporations are sensitive to the psychological/symbolic connection between personal identities and "consumer goods," and they design "commercials" exploiting this connection. If people want to be considered "in" or "hip," they will have to buy and wear a certain pair of pants or shirt or shoes. In order to attract someone, they should use a particular shampoo, perfume, or deodorant. If consumers want to attract positive attention, they'll have to own products that evoke this sentiment—for example, the most popular automobile, or computer, or a mansion on the beach.

The meaning of life in most technologically developed cultures on Earth seems to be this: Work hard, make money, and then spend it. In fact, the importance of "work" is revealed in the language these humans use to describe their daily routine. They divide their time into two general categories—"work" and "off work." Most humans "work" 8 to 10 (or more) hours a day for at least five days out of a seven-day week. After "work" and on the weekends humans are usually "off."

During this "off" time humans are *free*; their time is theirs to do with as they wish. However, after eight or more hours of "work" during the weekday the "off" occurs at a time of low energy levels and cannot last long. Some working humans yearn for the weekends—"thank God it's Friday"—when they are *free* for two days. During this time, they may *relax*, or they may *play*.

On the other hand, references to "work" in general tend to reflect a disquieting or even negative attitude, as if "jobs" were an unpleasant obligation. While engaged in "work" they were no longer *free*. Our reports note that only a small percentage of humanity really loves their "work"; others must tolerate their "jobs" with pride and enjoyment or shame and embarrassment.

However, we want to point out there are many different categories of "work," and these differences seem to be divided globally by north and south Most of the technologically "developed" countries are concentrated in the northern hemisphere and tend to exploit the people and natural resources of the southern hemisphere. There are great disparities. We observed cobalt mines in Africa where human children as young as eight "worked" under near-slavery conditions, sometimes paid a dollar a day. Giant corporations based in the north use the cobalt to produce electronic objects and sell them at great profit, usually to consumers in the north. The consequences of this imbalance between north and south are evident in rates of poverty, health conditions, education, political repression, and warfare.

The general division of daily life into "work" and "off" occurs because most humans are *employees*, which means they work for someone else, typically a corporation or government bureaucracy. According to our historical research, this situation contrasts starkly from conditions in the late eighteenth century. At that time, the central features of the cultural landscape consisted of independent individuals trading with one another—offering a special skill or owning a piece of land for production. Usually, land was passed onto the next generation; special skills were taught to *apprentices*. Working for someone else for wages often carried a faint connotation of desperation or "hard luck," and hopefully was only a temporary condition.

Now, however, many citizens around the world hope to become "employees" and "make a living." This transition is

striking; earlier ideas about wage labor carried negative connotations, and yet today wage labor is regarded as acceptable
and desirable—indeed, necessary, because "money" is necessary for survival. Although humans express a sense of *captivity*
to their "jobs," they say the words "work" and "off work" with
little recognition or reflection of the deeper meanings. They
take for granted that they must devote most of their life to
"work," like it or not, and cherish the "off" time when they are
free. Somewhere in this process lies a conundrum, but we can't
quite see it—only the shape of it.

It is impossible to discuss the sellers of consumption
without exploring the role of Earth's media. The most popular media—television—is an elaborate sales tool, supported
by advertisements for "consumer goods and services." Radio
and the Internet are also supported by commercials for products. In fact, the history of mass media in the United States
is closely related to the story of public relations and corporate
promotional campaigns.

Our investigations revealed that Edward Bernays, President Woodrow Wilson's wartime propaganda chief, was one of
the first to recognize the power and potential of mass communications. Applying principles derived from social scientists,
including his uncle, Sigmund Freud, Bernays enjoyed huge
success in turning public opinion against the "terrible Hun"
(the German enemy). In a fit of idealism, he saw social utopia
on the horizon—governments could use the mass media to
mold the minds of their citizens and ensure acquiescence and
compliance.

Bernays worked with radio and print media, which had
just begun to reach out on a national level. Corporations took
immediate notice; the power of mass marketing could work
even better for the private sector.

Early radio programs were liberally seeded with commercials—usually for the products made or sold by the "sponsor"

of the program, a corporate entity. We've listened to tapes of programs from the 1930s and '40s. The commercials were quite elaborate, delivering tiny periods of entertainment, with full-piece orchestras and choirs singing their joy and amazement. Some corporate trademark names became U.S. cultural icons, even recognized globally; Coca-Cola, Lucky-Strike, Camel, Ford, and Chevrolet.

The introduction of television in the 1950s created a revolution in mass communications. The impact of TV was far more powerful than radio. Quickly, commercials for "consumer goods" became a regular feature of all TV programming and soon were taken for granted by the viewing audience.

TV offers programming that allegedly delivers entertainment—such as, drama, sit-coms, "game shows," and news, while commercials offer "consumer goods and services." Although the viewing audience may distinguish a program as fiction or non-fiction (or sports), the commercials are recognized as a sales pitch. Commercials are designed to capture the viewer's attention and make a point. They tend to combine non-fiction and fantasy and usually ignore literal truth.

For example, commercials aimed toward younger humans often feature popular cartoon characters that exist only in the imagination. Tony the Tiger, the "image" of a popular breakfast cereal, conveys to youngsters that if they eat enough Sugar Frosted Flakes, they'll hit the baseball farther. This is clearly untrue, but such claims are made routinely. (In Latin American countries, Tony el Tigre is a soccer whiz.) In another example, we are told that the fragrance of a particular shampoo will attract beautiful people and romance is possible.

Humans (consumers) tend to identify with the characters appearing in these commercials, even though they're paid actors reciting from a script (or cartoon images). We recognize a definite connection between viewers and the commercials. The constant exposure and repetition of product names and corporate logos sinks into the subconscious and triggers reflexes. Social psychologists and corporate research departments understand this process. Consumers are manipulated and conditioned every day, and not only by the visual/audio media.

The lay-out of most supermarkets, for instance, is the result of careful research. As shoppers first enter, they encounter the sights and smells of fresh fruits and vegetables. Ostensibly, this is real food: organic, straight from the Earth! This induces what researchers call "the pastoral effect"—shoppers are charmed and uplifted and enter the packaged area of the store in the proper mood.

The aisles are wide, the lighting is bright but indirect, and music filters down from speakers in the ceiling. The music will usually be instrumental or even classical—both of which tend to make people spend a little more.

Corporations pay rent to the supermarket for prime shelf space. Eye-level is considered the best. The lower shelves are the low-rent district. The highest rents are charged for the butts of aisles, which are the biggest selling locations, and often feature high-profit items (like giant soft drink bottles) or special sales.

The kitchen essentials (such as milk, eggs, cheese, meat, and juice) tend to be located toward the back of the store, forcing quick-stop customers to walk through the aisle system and the tempting gauntlet of goodies. Our reports show that shoppers dropping by for only three or four items usually buy six or seven.

Humans respond to these subtle cues. Such stimuli appear to slip directly into the subconscious and trigger predictable impulses. Although the physical arrangement of a supermarket is a passive medium, it has a powerful effect on human behavior.

With supermarkets, the mode of manipulation is the lay-out and "ambience" of interior space. With television, the manipulation is audio/visual images. "Entertainment programs" are tailor-made for the different "time-slots" of each day, according to the expected audience (consumers), and commercials are tailor-made for each particular audience. For example, cartoon characters appear in commercials most often on Saturday morning because this "time-slot" is targeted at children.

Commercials are designed to manipulate, and they do so in an obvious way. Humans know a commercial when they see one, and they can watch it, ignore it, or click it off.

However, the entertainment programs—"dramas" and "sit-coms"—also manipulate, but in a more subtle and insidious manner; the manipulation appears as "background" and slips easily into the human mind. The houses the characters live in, their furniture and decoration, the clothes, jewelry, and ornaments they wear, their physical characteristics, the cars they drive, the money they make, the lovers they love—all these are cues to a conventional consumerist lifestyle, no matter what the "story" or theme of the program.

In an effort to attract consumers to watch programs, the media creates and presents "stars"—public personalities who attract the attention of millions. These movie and TV stars entice viewers to watch programs and buy the products they promote.

Media celebrities occupy a special niche in consumerist activity. They employ carefully orchestrated public relations strategies, usually appear in public immaculately groomed, wearing the latest name-brand fashions (or nothing at all) and presenting a positive, friendly attitude. Millions of "fans" elevate the identities of these stars to "larger-than-life" images. They are admired, followed, and imitated. This increases the "value" of their image, and they often sell their images to corporate advertisers. This is most evident in the connection between professional sports and product promotion. Some athletic stars, for example, earn more income from "promotional activities" than from their regular salaries.

Many U.S. citizens are proud to claim they have no aristocrats or royalty, and yet they create the equivalents with Hollywood stars, rock stars, or sports stars—such as Marilyn Monroe, Elvis, Michael Jackson, Madonna, and Ronaldo. These celebrities were and are still well-known, well-regarded, and "loved" by millions. Although the U.S. revolution included a repudiation of aristocracy, it appears that the media has created functional equivalents.

However, when celebrities commit some social sin or scandal, the public and the media are likely to strike back, switching quickly from love to loathing, destroying the celebrities' images and sometimes their lives. There are plenty of examples. Again, this is most evident in sports, when sports heroes suddenly behave badly or commit a "crime." Big corporations, worried about their "image," will immediately distance themselves from disgraced stars, and many of the public will follow with their condemnation. In our observation, some people often behave like overgrown children playing with blocks; it seems fun to stack them up, but much more fun to watch them tumble down!

This strikes us as a strange phenomenon; humans create heroes and then tear them to pieces. The tearing down of famous characters delivers a strong dose of passion and drama—not unlike the lynch parties and witch burnings of earlier times. We assume this is a form of "real-time" social theater, with the electronic media as stage and spotlight, and most of the population as actors and audience. To the participants in this ongoing societal theater, the passion and action seem "real."

In most countries on Earth the media industry is a corporate enterprise. The media outlet is a corporation; the programs are produced and sponsored by corporations; the commercials are made and presented by corporations; the "consumer goods" are produced and sold by corporations. It's not surprising that the attitudes of corporate boards (mostly non-minority males) are reflected in their design and choice of programming. This is not the result of any secret plan or conspiracy. Corporate boards and the owners (not always the same people) occupy similar social positions with similar interests and values — including their emphasis on self-preservation. Also, these "creators" of television programs (and owners of the corporations) are themselves shaped and molded by the dominant values and beliefs within the Cultural Model.

Corporate promotional departments employ armies of statisticians, psychologists, and sociologists to study the TV audience and break it down according to age group, education, income level, geographic location, and myriad other demographic factors. Commercials are carefully crafted toward the interests and tastes of all likely audiences.

It is not surprising, therefore, that commercials tend to reflect prevailing attitudes, prejudices, and stereotypes. Commercials for products and services related to the kitchen or laundry, for example, typically feature a conservatively dressed woman, since this is her "place" or "role" in the home. On the other hand, commercials for cars, beer, or tools—designed to appeal mostly to men—also feature women, but often half-naked. Clowns, happy kids, and cartoon characters dominate commercials targeted toward children.

Television not only reflects popular culture, but also creates it, shapes it, and reinforces it. Promotional departments seize the symbols and language of emerging social movements and turn them into sales strategies. In this process, cultural quirks become cleaned-up, sanitized, and no longer quirky. This may be regarded as "homogenizing the culture." Moreover, this process may encourage the constant drive to find something "new."

Because of the superficial nature of television, information is presented in quick, short-hand form. These "sound bites" reduce complex issues and arguments into short slogans, which may sound good to some people but carry no information. Along with the consumerist ideals promoted by television, this reductionism of information is equally damaging to the social and physical environment. Although relatively new social media outlets such as Facebook, YouTube, Twitter, and Instagram challenge this reductionism, the corporate media appears to be trying to marginalize such challenges.

These intractable problems of television via the corporate media were addressed brilliantly by Jerry Mander in his book *The Four Arguments for the Elimination of Television* (1978). Mander, a former advertising executive, argues that the broadcasting content of TV creates a mental condition among the viewers that is favorable for autocratic control by the political leadership. Television sells not only "consumer goods" but also political and social values. Further, television is a corporate creation and not "democratic." Access to television broadcasting is strictly controlled, and the viewing public is exposed to only those programs and political opinions within the boundaries of the status quo—that is, a mainstream interpretation of "reality."

According to Mander (1978), television content has important effects. "[The effects] organize society in a certain way. They give power to a very small number of people to speak into the brains of almost everyone else in the system night after night after night, with images that make people turn out in a certain kind of way. It affects the psychology of people who watch. It increases the passivity of people who watch. It changes family relationships. It changes understandings of nature. It flattens perception so that information, which you need a fair amount of complexity to understand it as you would get from reading, this information is flattened down to a much reduced form on television" (p. 49).

The commercials and programs on television are geared toward promoting a consumerist lifestyle and delineating political boundaries. This promotion is centered on conformity and the competitive nature of consumption.

We are puzzled by this constant consumption—high and low. It appears that the majority of humans spend most of their waking hours engaged in "work" so they may consume, and that this consumption is not merely to survive, but also to purchase "goods" that confer ranking, status, and comfort. Furthermore, the distribution of consumption is grossly unbalanced and out of proportion to the population; almost a third of humans consume very little or almost nothing, while barely 1 percent own or control more than half the world's wealth. Also, with the continuous extraction of resources to provide all the things consumers "demand," humans inflict great damage on their world. These extraction efforts waste an enormous amount of carbon energy, but they also destroy habitats—not only plants and animals, but also people. There are currently many confrontations occurring in different parts of the Earth between private "developers" and indigenous peoples defending their traditional homeland. Here again we see the shadow of absurdity; the drive to consume leads to environmental and social disaster.

Now we consider a slightly different aspect of consumption, one that lies deep beneath the sellers and assemblers; the extraction of raw materials and resources. Nearly everything humans buy comes from the Earth, including, of course, the "necessities" of life—food and shelter—but also the glut of "consumer goods." This process means that natural eco-systems are disturbed or destroyed to satisfy the "demands" of the human consumer.

All inhabitants of Earth's eco-system—fauna and flora, tiny and big—have evolved together according to the planet's atmospheric and material conditions. These primary elements determine the complex, finely-balanced self-sustaining whole, with all life-forms intricately connected to each other, to the local weather pattern, and to the atmosphere. Further, these components give and take from each other in a cooperative/competitive feedback process of survival.

In this regard, we make a curious observation; in the "modern," urban cultures, humans consider themselves *apart* from nature, which of course they are physically, with all the concrete and asphalt, but they are also apart psychologically and in their personal identification. On the other hand, people in indigenous cultures tend to become *integrated* with nature—equal partners with the trees, the animals, the mountains, the lakes, and the weather. Many indigenous people express their deep connection to the environment by usually referring to all creation, including themselves, as "children of Mother Earth."

We discovered a book by Vine Deloria, a noted American Indian scholar and author. He wrote this: "If all things are related, the unity of creation demands that each life-form contribute its intended contribution. Any violation of another entity's right to existence is a violation of the nature of creation and a degradation of religious reality itself" (Deloria 1973:299). He goes on to stress that humans can't take a walk in nature because humans are part of nature, despite their current attempts to view nature as something to control or tame. This indigenous world view is strikingly at odds with the present dominant global perspective, which regards Earth's ecosystem as both resource and trash container.

Earth's finely-tuned, global ecosystem is highly vulnerable to the slightest changes in the atmosphere; for example, the approximate 1.5 degree (Fahrenheit) rise in global temperature over the last century has already disturbed multitudes of local eco-systems, and if it rises only one more degree, the earth might face catastrophic consequences. Since 1957, the Mauna Lao Observatory in Hawaii has recorded carbon dioxide levels in the atmosphere. Recently, for the first time, the level of CO_2 passed over 400 parts per million, and it continues to climb.

The data and analysis indicate that carbon dioxide levels in the Earth's atmosphere are definitely rising, and higher levels of CO_2 mean more heat. This is a cause and effect sequence that obeys the laws of physics and chemistry, despite human beliefs and opinions. Most of the commentary we've seen—for and against—cannot change this chemical/atomic relationship. Global warming on Earth is a fact, and humans bear a great amount of the responsibility.

The consequences of this warming, however, are indeed controversial; we and the humans have little idea of what to expect. It seems that the Earth and all its inhabitants have moved into a new phase of existence, one with rapid change occurring among the most basic elements of survival. Climate scientists and their computer models are constantly surprised by nature's "real time" behavior; their predictions are too high, too low, or too irregular. Although the future of global warming is hazy, the most extreme predictions are frightening; the melting of the world's glaciers and Polar Regions, rising sea levels, changing weather patterns, food shortages, and the movement and extinction of species—including humans.

The issue of climate change continues to swirl with controversy, obfuscation, and downright fabrication. Since the relationship between carbon and heat is quite simple and natural, we can only conclude this controversy is related to fear, denial, and ignorance—and the ignorance is not simply absence of knowledge, but a *deliberate* ignorance.

In his book *Agnotology: The Making and Unmaking of Ignorance* (2007), Robert Proctor focuses on types of ignorance: "There must be as many kinds of ignorance as of knowledge—perhaps more, given how scant is our knowledge compared to the vastness of our ignorance.... The focus here is on ignorance—or doubt or uncertainty—as something that is made, maintained, and manipulated by means of certain arts and sciences" (p. 3).

In the case of global warming and climate change, much of the doubt and confusion is stirred up by sectors of the economy with a special interest in maintaining the current dependence on fossil fuels and carbon-based energy. They manage the ignorance campaign with non-profit "think tanks" and "institutes," along with the mass media; they lobby and influence political leaders to pass favorable legislation and discourage alternative energy programs. A similar "ignorance" campaign had been waged earlier by the tobacco industry—submitting mountains of "data" and "scientific reports" challenging the idea that smoking can cause cancer. Later, it was discovered this "ignorance" campaign was deliberately misleading—a "smokescreen," ironically. Nevertheless, these doubts—coupled with the addictive properties of tobacco—were enough to encourage millions of smokers to keep buying cigarettes. Now the doubts and confusion about global warming encourage people to keep consuming petroleum—which may also be addictive—and ignore alternative technologies.

In addition, humans are reluctant to face head-on the serious possibility that their consumerist activities are having a profound effect on Earth's health and well-being, and therefore their own survival. Although they have convened several global conferences and signed several international accords and promises, most countries—and in particular their consumers—don't appear to regard reduction of consumption as a serious necessity. It appears that consumption is *accelerating*, and will continue to accelerate as more countries intensify their efforts toward "development."

Global temperature change is a slow, innocuous process, and although it is gradual, its effects will be considerable, and are already in evidence. The Arctic ice cover is at its lowest level in recent history and continues melting. Iceland and Antarctica also experience extreme melting. Compare this gradual process to the sheer violence and immediacy of hundreds of chainsaws clear-cutting the Amazon forest. Both these processes, the innocuous and the violent, are triggered by corporate voracity and human consumerist behavior.

These social and environmental conditions mystify us. Earth is one of the most beautiful, richest planets we've ever seen, and yet the inhabitants treat their world quite badly—stripping away the eco-systems to make "products," then throwing away the "products" when they become "trash," damaging the world even further!

The current expansion of the global human population, along with expanded corporate interests, has led to a powerful impact on global ecosystems, primarily in extraction of raw materials. For example, the Trans Amazonian highway, built into the Brazilian rainforest, has led to the continuous destruction of a highly diverse, necessary component of Earth's ecosphere, as well as the people who live there.

In this case, the invasion of the Amazon is focused on a search for precious minerals and to clear land for crops and pastures—that is, in the interests of profit and consumption. Here we see another glimpse into absurd behavior, for the Amazon rainforest is a crucial component of Earth's eco-system!

We discovered an award-winning book entitled *Ishmael* by Daniel Quinn. The story contains an informative dialogue about "Takers" and "Leavers." The Takers are the non-indigenous populations digging away at the world's resources. However, the indigenous people, the Leavers, are described this way: "Each Leaver people has a system that works well for them because it *evolved* among them; it was suited to the terrain in which they lived, suited to the climate in which they lived, suited to the biological community in which they lived, suited to their own peculiar tastes, preferences, and vision of the world" (Quinn 1992:119).

Leavers are as much a part of the Brazilian rainforest as the trees. When Takers move into more remote regions of the Earth, searching and extracting, disturbing and destroying ecosystems, they also disturb and destroy the people who live there. According to the wise Ishmael, the main difference between Takers and Leavers is this: "Takers accumulate knowledge about what works well for *things*. Leavers accumulate knowledge about what works well for *people*" (Quinn 1992:219).

Human population growth has exploded in recent decades. There are over seven billion humans on Earth today, and in the next 10 years there might be one billion more. How will the humans clothe, house, and feed those billions, plus produce a myriad of "consumer goods?" They often take from the Earth what they want; treating it as though it was their private property to do with as they wish, irrelevant of the consequences, and then throw the "products" back to the Earth when they become "trash."

Undoubtedly, part of this over-exploitation of global resources is motivated by sheer desperation and hunger—similar to the motives behind the decimation of the Haitian rainforest. In the poorest country in the Western Hemisphere, people stripped the Earth to feed themselves. However, by far the greatest amount of ecological damage is devoted to two giant intertwined enterprises—production of "consumer goods" and extraction of "strategic materials."

We are not unduly alarmed at this rapid growth in human population. We believe the Earth is still so rich in resources it has the potential to provide the necessities—food, housing, clothing—for the entire world's people. However, we also note that the mysterious mechanism in the distribution of these resources is so grossly uneven that nearly a third of humanity lives in abject poverty.

We are alarmed at the rapidly changing global eco-systems and the devastating effects of these changes on the Earth's ecology. According to our calculations, Earth is currently experiencing a significant extinction event in both flora and fauna, and although most of this is due to human expansion, there are other strange, unintended consequences. For example, in an effort to make it easier to clean and care for catfish farms in the southern United States, Asian carp were introduced as scavengers. These fish escaped the catfish farms, invaded the Mississippi River and are now closing in on the Great Lakes. They eat more than the native fish, grow bigger, reproduce more rapidly, and have no natural predators. In fact, the Asian carp are driving the native fish to extinction, and if they ever get into the Great Lakes they would cause an ecological catastrophe. Researchers have tried to control the carp, from poison to dynamite, but apart from killing everything else as well, these methods have not stopped the carp from moving closer to Chicago's canals.

There are plenty of other examples of humans introducing alien species into unfamiliar ecosystems, sometimes intentionally, sometimes not. These new species either die off or assimilate; other times they upset the finely-balanced rhythms and cause havoc.

The human activity of mass consumption may be regarded as the behavior of a sick species, since it has brought Earth to the brink of disaster. Some of our reports suggest that this suicidal behavior might be an unconscious, instinctual response to the population growth—that is, designed to kill off a significant part of the human population before the humans kill the Earth. On the other hand, if there is no underlying logical basis, and the humans are simply engaged in blind, unconcerned consumption, then this is most puzzling.

Finally, no discussion of consumption is complete without acknowledging the ending phase of consumption; that is, "trash." Most "consumer goods" that humans buy and use are eventually "thrown away."

Obviously, the eco-system is damaged by extracting resources to make products, then the discarded products are returned to the Earth, but they are returned radically altered by the process of "production"—oftentimes toxic. Human-controlled corporations take natural resources and turn some into poisonous materials, especially plastic. Most consumer products come in a package of plastic, paper, or cardboard and these materials become trash. Also, the products will eventually become trash, no matter how long they last.

The largest component of trash in the world is plastic. Plastic is a petroleum byproduct, highly toxic to the Earth and typically has a break-down life of hundreds of years. The only scientifically recognized way to break down plastic is via photo-degradation; exposure to UV rays breaks bonds, turning larger pieces of plastic into smaller ones. In the United States, consumers "throw away" over *one hundred billion* plastic bags a year, while barely 1 percent is recycled (Profita, 2013). Home to approximately 4 percent of the global population, U.S. citizen's account for more than 30 percent of the planet's total waste generation. (This not only measures the level of trash but also the level of *consumption*.) Each American discards an average of more than 1,650 pounds of garbage every year, or approximately 4.6 pounds per person per day. Most of this "trash" is stored "forever" in municipal "landfills," or "thrown away" into the ocean, or exported to countries such as China, where it is supposedly reused.

Especially troubling, from our view, are the many products designed as "disposable"—they are made to work once or a few

times, then "thrown away." This was another brilliant marketing strategy introduced in the 1960s—razors, cigarette lighters,
diapers, paper towels, and hundreds of other products began
to be made and sold cheaply because they were not meant to
last. And since these products were made for the "trash," people
would have to continually purchase new ones—and continually
"throw them away."

We'll use the following example from the U.S., but it is
generally true in most countries. During the 1950s most families had relied on soft cotton cloth diapers, which were used
and washed over and over again. Then, during the explosion
of market segmentation and "personalized" products, plastic
coated disposable diapers arrived on the scene, boasting of
"convenience, comfort, and speed." They came with cute, heart-
tugging names: Pampers, Huggies, Luvs. They're designed
to be used once, then "thrown away," and they are—over 20
billion dirty diapers a year wind up in U.S. "landfills," nearly
four million tons of waste. It's the same in most other countries. These dirty diapers are essentially raw sewage wrapped
in plastic, a particularly lethal brew.

Of more immediate danger and harm are the billions of
plastic disposable lighters bought, used and "thrown away."
Although billions of these lighters also wind up in "landfills,"
we'll use an example from the perspective of the ocean. Seat-
tle-based photographer Chris Jordan (www.chrisjordan.com,
p. 9) has documented the bird population of Midway Atoll,
two thousand miles from any continent but not far from the
Great Pacific Gyre (rotating current), which is now known
as the Great Pacific Garbage Patch. His powerful images are
grim testimony to the harmful effects of consumer "trash" on
habitats and animals living far from "civilization." He found
thousands of albatross chicks dead from eating human "trash,"
most of it plastic that their parents had picked up in the ocean
and fed to them as "food."

Based on Jordan's photographs, one of the biggest killers of chicks are disposable plastic cigarette lighters. They float, shine in the sun, and are easy targets, as are all small pieces of plastic. He displays dozens of photos of dead chicks with their stomachs exposed and filled with colorful plastic—lighters, bottle caps, and pieces of bags. This is another wretched unintended consequence of consumer activity—drama and death among the albatross. Equally disturbing, this drama is nearly invisible to the humans who cause it, as is mostly "trash" activity.

Most humans are well aware of the many Chinese products exported into the United States, but not many know that one of the biggest U.S. exports to China is trash. Recycling plastic in the United States is expensive and not "cost-effective"; it's much easier to load it on giant container ships and send it over to the Chinese, who buy and reuse some of it.

For the last several years the United States has exported billions of tons of plastic waste to China, taking the pressure off domestic "landfills," but also dampening political efforts at passing recycling laws. Moreover, this gigantic trash export to other countries such as China has not encouraged investment in recycling centers in the United States, and has essentially moved the trash problem from one side of the world to the other.

Trash troubles, however, are brewing on the horizon. China has been forced to face its environmental woes and take concrete steps to stem the damage (mainly for political reasons and social control). The Chinese government launched "Operation Green Fence" in 2012, which bans imports of certain types of waste, including unwashed plastics or illegal waste, such as syringes mixed in with the plastic. According to Oregon Public Broadcasting (June 2013), truckloads of plastic were stacking up at Oregon recycling depots, unable to unload. Apparently, many Chinese buyers cancelled their orders. In the years after implementation of the new rules, China's Green Fence policy impacted the recycling industry across the globe. U.S. exporters have had to clean up their systems, and most recyclers are producing a much higher quality material. Another side effect of the policy is that many small companies in China who had been dealing with dirty recycling have gone out of business or been bought out or consolidated by larger firms. The impact of the process of monopolization of the industry is on-going.

As landfills are filling with trash, the Earth's oceans are also filling with trash—again, most of it plastic. Oceanographers have identified five major ocean currents in the world, all moving in a particular direction according to a combination of wind, sea, electro-magnetic forces, and the Earth's rotation. One of the biggest of these ocean currents—in fact, the largest eco-system on Earth—is the Great Pacific Gyre. However, as mentioned earlier, oceanographers now refer to this current as the Great Pacific Garbage Patch.

Plastics, chemical debris, and everything imaginable swirls around in a gigantic slow-motion circle, thousands of miles long, and with each revolution it picks up more and more trash from several countries and continents. Further, this is a closed system; the trash rarely escapes, and since most of the trash is non-biodegradable, it constantly accumulates. Scientists have collected over 750,000 bits of plastic in one square kilometer of the "garbage patch."

Plastic in the ocean breaks down into finer and finer particles, spreading toxins over a wide area and to considerable depth. The consequences to the eco-system have been dramatic, not only to the larger marine life—fishes and birds—but also to sensitive organisms like plankton and algae, which are essential to the entire food chain. The tiny particles of plastic block and deflect the sun's energy (gamma) rays that feed these basic nutrients, and these nutrients feed everything else—all the way up to whales. There is also a similar garbage patch circulating in the North Atlantic. These garbage patches are a direct result of detrimental corporate and human consumerist behavior.

When we combine the effects of giant "garbage patches" with the effects of overfishing, we see dramatic changes in the quality and population of marine life. Overfishing, or illegal fishing—including stealing the eggs of endangered turtles—is related directly to consumption. Also, there are the effects from global warming. For example, the Great Barrier Reef off Australia is slowly dying from changes in water temperature, along with the dumping of pollutants. Here again, the Reef is a breeding ground for thousands of species. As the Reef dies, other species will dwindle and die, triggering a domino effect throughout the food chain.

This squandering and destruction of vital resources is an alien concept to us. Our home world is small and cold and poor in resources, but it's our *home* and we regard every resource as precious. When we first arrived at Earth, we were charmed and excited by its beauty, diversity, and abundance. In fact, we admit to feeling a bit of envy. Now, however, we are shocked and confused. Incredibly, the humans are rapidly depleting the abundance of their world, which will, of course, deplete *them*.

There are signs of sensible change; more countries invest in sustainable sources of energy, such as wind and solar, but these efforts might be too little and too late. But even these "alternative" energy sources are highly dependent on carbon-based energy—in the manufacture, transport and assembly of solar panels or windmills; in the mining of materials and manufacture of giant battery banks. Moreover, the conversion to alternative energies is greatly hindered by the political power of the present producers of energy—petroleum, coal, and nuclear.

We observed that some advocates of the "green movement"—promoting "alternative energy"—are infused with the attitude that technology will provide enough energy to maintain present levels of consumption. This infusion suggests humans may continue with their consumerist lifestyles, and need only change the manner of extraction and use of energy. Yet, continuous consumption is *unsustainable*. The Earth is a wholly contained organism, an island in space, with limited resources and a finely tuned ecosphere. But humans are fast depleting and destroying the resources, and driving the ecosphere into mass extinction.

The inertia of damage will continue into the near future. Global temperatures will continue to rise for the next few decades, even if humans stop all carbon emissions immediately. Equally disheartening, it will take the Earth several hundreds or even thousands of years to recover, if it ever does. Nevertheless, we calculate that if the humans introduce revolutionary changes immediately, they have a chance to save their world and themselves and their children.

The consumerist philosophy permeates all facets of human experience. Of course, there is consumption as survival, which is the mode of living for nearly a third of humans. But there is also the consumption of "consumer goods and services," which supply wealthier peoples with not only comfort and convenience but also power, prestige and status.

Connected to this consumerist activity are a myriad of auxiliary activities, chief of which are "education" and "work." There are also the creators and producers of "consumer goods," which must disturb or destroy ecosystems to get at the resources. The "remains" of the packaged products contribute to the gigantic amount of "trash" deposited all over the Earth. Finally, there are the unknown dangers and effects of global warming, which the Earth is just beginning to experience.

This continuous assault against Earth's ecology is the responsibility of every human being. They have brought their home to dangerous levels of stress with unknown consequences. Therefore, since the damage is global, people on Earth have essentially transcended their national/ethnic identities to assume their Prime Identity: Earthling.

Most of our observations regarding the above discussion were concentrated on the wealthy segment of the human population, which is the minority. At least 80 percent of all humans live on $10 or less a day, and $10 a day does not allow much purchasing of "consumer goods." Therefore, only about 20 percent of Earth's population (concentrated in the northern hemisphere) can afford to continually purchase "consumer goods" and services, including "luxury" goods. However, we want to stress that it is this minority that consumes most of Earth's resources and "throws away" most of the trash.

This wildly uneven distribution of consumption results in startling extremes in living conditions and survival potential. For example, people in the United States "throw away" nearly forty million tons of food a year—the biggest component of trash in municipal "landfills"—while millions of people in Sub-Saharan Africa suffer from malnutrition and starvation. In fact, there is even malnutrition in the United States. Yet, according to our calculations, the Earth produces enough food for all humans.

How can such a gross discrepancy occur, and, even more interesting, why is it allowed to continue? Our preliminary conclusion is that the manner and structure of distribution must be faulty or incomplete. In our search for clues, we noticed that most of the poor and hungry humans are of distinct ethnic backgrounds, the pigmentation of their skin is brown or dark brown—again located mostly in the southern hemisphere—while most wealthy humans have a lighter complexion—and live in the north.

Why should these ethnic/geographic differences translate into such vast differences in lifestyle and the availability of resources for survival? So far, this remains a mystery. However, we know such differences must be significant because the same phenomena occur within countries, most noticeably in the wealthier countries.

According to our investigations, there is nothing remarkable in the physical and mental characteristics among different ethnic groups—intelligence levels, physical abilities, and emotional ranges are virtually identical for all humans. Therefore, the causes in the ranking of ethnic experience must be *social* and *political*.

Currently, the difference in consumption levels between the minority rich and everyone else is growing quite rapidly, with more people falling below the poverty line and more wealth concentrated in the hands of the rich. The most striking symbolism of these differences is found in the realities on the ground. We visited "towns" in Sub-Saharan Africa where people supposedly lived on the equivalent of less than two dollars a day. This is barely enough to sustain life, but not enough to stave off the effects of chronic malnutrition—such as sickness and disease.

The "houses" were most often canvas tents, supplied by world relief organizations, or simple structures made from organic materials. Crowded social conditions and poor health services often led to starvation and disease. The children were the most vulnerable and suffered a high rate of illness and death. There were no grocery stores, no movies, no malls, no restaurants, no big screen televisions, no sound systems, and no running water. These humble housing structures were devoid of "consumer goods." The people did not "work" or "produce goods," and the land around them appeared barren and used up. They only hoped to consume enough calories to make it through one more day.

We know these observations will be difficult to believe and even more difficult to understand, especially since Earth is so rich in natural resources. However, we are reporting exactly what we have seen. Obviously, a huge disconnect exists in the social dynamics of resource distribution.

From a global perspective, such conditions appear striking and obvious. Ethnic, pigmentation and gender differences seem relevant in this process, but the causes and motives remain obscure. Further, similar conditions exist on a smaller scale in many of the more affluent countries.

For example, we focused on wealth distribution in the United States, the richest country on Earth. According to census data and other sources, last year there were forty-six million people living below the "poverty line," which is defined as an annual income of $23,000 or less for a family of four. This was 15 percent of the population and a new, sad record (Census Bureau Current Population Survey [CPS, 2015], Annual Social and Economic Supplement [ASEC]). Apparently, the United States suffered recently from an economic "recession" and has not entirely recovered. Underemployment is still high, and wages remain stagnant. Yet, here again, we find evidence of ethnic issues; poverty rates for people labeled as minorities are often three times higher than those for others. Similar social conditions exist in countries in Europe.

Since all ethnicities have similar abilities, these conditions indicate a *structural* feature to the distribution of wealth and consumption. Also, the same uneven distribution typically exists between male and female humans, regardless of ethnicity or pigmentation; the ratios in salaries and promotions, for example, are consistently unequal—in favor of men (Bureau of Labor Statistics, May 2014).

Sexism and racism have deep roots in human history (Cruit, 2014). Humans often demonstrate a measure of fear and hesitancy regarding other humans of different color or physical characteristics. In the case of sexism, there are the obvious differences in biology, and these differences have usually evolved into divisions of labor between the sexes.

The social construct of "racism" is the categorizing or defining of particular ethnic groups in relation to one's own group. As we mentioned earlier, following the hegemonic process, humans create "in" groups and "out" groups, usually along racial or gender lines. The "in" group defines a different ethnic group as "out" or inferior, and therefore it is acceptable to enslave, kill, or steal from the members of this "sub-species." This process was evident during the colonial periods in human history, when entire nations of people were controlled, used, and abused for the benefit of the "in" group, which was usually of different ethnic origins.

These colonial traditions have been carried forward to the present day. Almost all countries in the world have experienced racism in their history, and still do. For example, the U.S. began its expansion by exterminating Indians and enslaving Africans; Great Britain and other European countries maintained vast colonial "empires." The racist attitudes fostered during those times were passed on from generation to generation.

Although racism and slavery are now "illegal," racism still exists within all social structures and is especially ingrained in northern cultures. Africans and Indians are not equal participants in U.S. and European society. They are consistently toward the bottom in basic social indicators such as income, health, and education.

These racial attitudes and unequal results are not the result of any inherent differences among ethnic groups, but are created through the hegemonic process of *political and social manipulation.* No humans are born sexist or racist—they learn these attitudes from the culture around them. Millions of people from a particular ethnic origin are suppressed, ignored, and denied, because it serves political and economic interests (Shabazz, 2015).

Sexism transcends almost all ethnic groups and is not primarily "racial." Biological differences evolved early social constructs and attitudes related to survival, most often expressed in a division of labor.

In many early isolated "pagan" societies—we use "pagan" in its original meaning, as "people of the forest"—the life-giving properties of women were considered sacred and related to the all-important concept of fertility. Fertility was vital for communities dependent on crops and animals. These early pagan communities, including indigenous peoples, formed ideas about the "supernatural" in which women often found a place as "goddesses" or "priestesses." Early Egyptian and Greek religions featured "goddesses" on an equal footing with "gods."

Maria Mies (1986) explains the drastic change in attitudes toward women with the rise of the world economy and patriarchy. Also, the growth of particular religious philosophies has resulted in the suppression and even "demonization" of women.

Consider the creation story in the Christian Bible; God made "Adam" from the original mud of the Earth, but he made "Eve" from the rib of "Adam." Eve was Adam's "mate" in the Garden of Eden. The serpent—the devil—seduced Eve and persuaded her to betray Adam and God. As a result, death, sickness, and sin descended on the world.

Other stories and references in the Bible reinforce this perspective of women as weak, tempestuous, and treacherous. Not even Mary, the mother of Jesus Christ, is considered a goddess, even though she was impregnated by God through the "Immaculate Conception." In fact, the most celebrated female in Christianity is a *virgin*. There are myriad other taboos and exclusions regarding women in Christianity, including the role of "priests" and the idea of "celibacy." Such attitudes continue to foster sexist behavior among Christians (and Western societies generally), but these attitudes are usually expressed in action—for example, unequal incomes and limited opportunities.

In Islam, another major religion on Earth, the differences in men and women are often presented more publically. The Koran articulates guidelines regarding dress and behavior between men and women, but the Koran, like the Bible, has been interpreted many different ways. There is a wide range of adherence to dogma. In some Islamic countries women are required to cover themselves—some from head to foot, with veils hiding their faces. In others, women adopt a more casual dress code. The more extreme sects deny women formal education or work opportunities. In Saudi Arabia, women have choices in dress and education, but are prohibited from driving vehicles, or walking alone in public. In most Islamic regions, men are the absolute rulers of the household (which might also be said of the Christian faith).

Again, there are essentially no differences between human men and women, apart from the biological. Therefore, sexism, like racism, is not an inherent component of "reality"—or even "divinity"—but only a social construct fostered and maintained through a hegemonic process of persuasion and intimidation, which starts at birth. For example, when a human baby is born, a typical first question is "is it a boy or a girl?" The answer will trigger whole vocabularies of motive and categories of behavior specific to that particular gender. Boy babies and girl babies are treated differently, and these differences will have a profound impact on the trajectory their lives.

Finally, we discovered another absurdity; within the norms of socialization human females are generally considered more compassionate, more intellectually open, and more courageous than males, and yet they are suppressed and sometimes abused.

In fact, in the U.S. there is a higher rate of women killed by men than of soldiers killed in combat.

We want to note a curious development directly related to technology. For decades the police have shot and killed "perpetrators" who had threatened them in some way. In most cases, the police justified their actions because they feared for their lives or the lives of others. However, with the proliferation of security cameras and cell phones with cameras, several videos have been recorded depicting police shooting and killing unarmed people. In some cases, these killings are clearly deliberate, and show police altering the evidence.

Several such incidents around the country provoked protests and demonstrations and encouraged the expansion of a broad-based movement called "Black Lives Matter." There are also movements for more accountability from the police. Among these proposals is a requirement for police to wear "body cameras" and film their own actions.

However, technology will not solve racism. In a racist culture, almost everyone born and raised will absorb racist attitudes. Police are especially vulnerable, mainly because they operate within a sort of feedback system that confirms and strengthens racism. Minorities usually have been pushed toward the bottom of social/economic life and forced to concentrate in particular residential areas with low rents and cheap housing. With little opportunity for "jobs" or quality education, "criminal activities" become attractive to many desperate people—and the police pursue "criminals," which often brings them into contact with minorities, and usually within a contentious context. (We contrast this with the "criminals" hidden inside giant corporations—the ones wearing "suits" working in "offices"—who steal millions in illicit profits, destroy ecosystems and push aside entire indigenous nations.)

In our estimation, racism and sexism are *social constructions* created by select groups of humans and diffused into the social structure through the economy, education, religion, and media. Such fantasies become realities benefitting most light-skinned males; however, the "hierarchy" spreads out the rewards unequally into the general population, which is how racism and sexism are perpetuated. Most people believe the facades.

Prejudice exists within the minds of humans, and is expressed and nourished within the world of informal social intercourse—that is, close friends, family, and associates. This network of informal social relationships exerts great influence in the application of the *formal* law: Laura Nader (2002) notes that although formal-legal structures prohibit sexual and racial discrimination, there is a difference between the law on the books versus law in action, as well as "mind-control." Racism and sexism were created initially by the manufacturers of consent and ignorance, and are now embedded within most formal and informal institutions. The resulting hierarchal order from these prejudices confers a clear advantage upon the political and economic leadership.

Consumption levels based on ethnicity and gender are an obvious element of Earth's social reality, not only in the distribution of wealth, but in market segmentation. By designating and maintaining "gender roles," manufacturers and advertisers open up endless opportunities for new products designed only for men and only for women. At the same time, through constant depiction and reinforcement of such gender "differences," men and women are conditioned to accept these differences as "natural" or "normal." In this way, gender discrimination can become a permanent feature of the social structure.

A larger, more general social status ranking exists in most countries on Earth, encompassing entire populations, regardless of ethnicity or gender. The shape of this ranking is pyramidal: The broad group at the bottom is composed of the poor and disadvantaged; higher up, within the narrower middle range, are those with employment and limited consumption choices; and perched at the top—the smallest population—are the rich and "superrich" with seemingly unlimited consumption opportunities.

This is only an outline, yet it reflects the general shape of the aggregate. There are no clear boundaries between these "classes," and movement is fairly fluid. However, the basic structure rarely changes. In this way, we see that the 10-20 percent of wealthy humans on Earth are composed of the top "classes" in each country, while most of the remaining 80-90 percent of humanity are distributed unevenly throughout the various "class structures." The only change in this structure is its *expansion*—that is, decreasing resources for the middle "class" and the poor, while more resources go to the wealthy.

During the last 35 years median family income, adjusted for inflation, has declined slightly, while income to the top 1 percent has increased over a 100 percent. It was reported that the income gap between rich and poor in the United States is the biggest it's been since the 1920s. This is generally true around the Earth. In January 2014 the World Economic Forum, one of the most influential economic organizations on Earth, warned in a press release that the growing gulf between the rich and the poor represents the biggest global risk in 2014: "The chronic gap between the incomes of the richest and poorest citizens is seen as the risk that is most likely to cause serious damage globally in the coming decade" (www.weforum.org, p. 19).

This finding was hard for us to believe since the wealth generated on Earth is enormous. Nevertheless, after checking with several sources, we concluded this gross imbalance truly exists. Equally important in our view is the finding that most humans born into a particular "class" tend to remain in that "class" for the rest of their lives. Most of those occupying the top class have inherited their position from the previous generation, or they are afforded advantages from social and political connections. In this way social mechanisms limit opportunities for those toward the bottom of the pyramid, while delivering greater advantages and access to those toward the top. This dynamic reveals a deeper level to this structure; it is not merely a "class" system but often also a "caste" system.

Aside from these wildly variable consumption levels, the total consumption of over seven billion humans, rich and poor, is rising steadily. There are "emerging economies" on Earth whose populations had previously been poor, but are now consuming at steadily higher levels and creating their own "class structures." Meanwhile, as the poor consume less, the rich consume much more.

Another intriguing phenomenon we noticed is that the poor and disadvantaged are also bombarded with messages to purchase "consumer goods," and they purchase what they can, usually at discount centers or on "credit," for which they pay steep interest rates. The impetus to consume is ingrained deeply into human consciousness, regardless of "social class," and we don't mean consumption as simple survival, but rather the idea to *consume as much as possible.* The irony in this social system is that the more one person consumes, the less is available for everyone else.

We can understand consumption as survival; however, consumption on a mass scale, including "luxury products," is still a puzzle to us. For example, recall the humble tent houses we saw in Sub-Saharan Africa and compare them with the "Presidential Suite" at The Ritz-Carlton Hotel in New York City. Both places are for sleeping and living, but the "Suite" has various "luxurious amenities" and costs over 3,000 dollars a night. Three thousand dollars would feed three tent families for a year, but only one person will sleep one night in the "Suite" and pay the bill, food not included.

Why pay so much? We've decided that whether it's recreation or business, most humans stay in the "Presidential Suite" to *make an impression*. Most often they want to maintain an image and impress others, yet at other times they seem inclined to impress themselves—as if reassuring themselves they are a "success." Here again, we encounter the symbolic nature of "luxury products."

Our task is to discover how it is that humans think this way. Formal laws and structures are relatively easily identified and form the visible side of social reality, but we know there is another, shadowy side to social reality — the network of informal associations that influence a person's choice of values, beliefs, and attitudes—life at home and on the streets. Although people may occupy formal positions, or no position, their performance is directly related to this internalized informal conversation.

The idea of consumption is a dominant force in most of the world's cultures, taught and encouraged in school and church, demonstrated daily by the routine workings of social reality—children work in schools; their parents work at "jobs." To investigate how humans acquire and transmit these ideas and beliefs, it is necessary to focus on education. Young children are extremely vulnerable to initial conditions and ideas, first among family and friends, but then they enter school and the entire culture is thrust on them—not only all its glory and good, but also the shame and evil. Young humans, as most other life-forms, usually absorb the culture(s) where they are born and raised.

CHAPTER 2: EDUCATION

The consumerist philosophy guides the primary focus of education in most cultures around the world. Children learn early in grade school to give up a portion of their time and energy in exchange for rewards or "advancements." In school, they earn "grades" and "diplomas"; later, after they graduate, they give up their time and energy to "work," where they earn the means to consume.

The transition from school to work is generally straight-forward. Children start kindergarten usually at five years old, and for the next 12 to 20 years they report in the morning to some school building or campus where they "work" and "learn," and then leave for home in the afternoon. When they graduate, they report in the morning for "work" at some building or office and then leave for home in the afternoon. If they are not independently wealthy, they are expected to perform this "work" for 40 or 45 years, when they usually "retire."

For many of the world's citizens, this broad, Cultural Model embraces their whole life experience, and many do not question or doubt the trajectory of this experience. They are born into a social and cultural structure that stresses conformity to the consumerist philosophy, and they absorb it quickly.

We identified a quiet turning point in the U.S. educational system, occurring about 100 years ago. The management of schools and school curricula were taken out of the hands of families and local communities and assumed by the federal government. Before this time, most schools in the U.S. and other countries consisted of classes of mixed-age students within a somewhat informal atmosphere, especially schools in rural areas. In an effort to "standardize" education on a national level, the government introduced a rigid, graduated system based on age. Children entered the system at a certain age, moved "forward" in a logical, sequential pattern and emerged as "graduates" ready for "work."

This primary school system was conceived in the social context of the early 1900s, when the industrial revolution was in full swing and "industry" was the driving force behind growth and prosperity. Especially admired was the highly successful "assembly-line" method of manufacturing. Also, the idea of "social engineering" was coming into vogue at this time, related directly to the burgeoning public relations industry.

The age-graduated school system strongly resembles an assembly-line approach to education: Students move in a linear, predetermined direction, picking up more information as they go, until, upon graduation, they are finally "finished products." For over 100 years, this has been the standard trajectory of most primary and secondary education.

For many young humans, the first day at school becomes an unforgettable experience, even traumatic. Suddenly, they're removed from their family and home and thrust into an unknown environment filled with strangers. They had heard about "school" from parents and day-care, but the reality of it is shocking.

In fact, this is the moment in most developed societies when children pass for the first time from the informal world of family into the formal world of centralized power structures. This is a crucial passage in the journey toward citizenship and total acceptance of "work" and consumerism.

Until this time, the main authority figures in a child's life are most likely parents or guardians and siblings, with "authority" rooted in affection and familiarity. However, the authority invested in school officials is something new for these children, something strange and distant—an intangible power rooted in the arrangement of formal identities: "Teachers" and "students."

The transition happens quickly, merely a matter of stepping into the school building, but we have calculated that the impact on children and the future trajectory of their lives is powerful. On the first day of school they encounter more fully the world of formal social control, including the focus on conformity and obedience.

Typically, Earth's formal institutions and bureaucracies are centralized power structures, with power flowing from top to bottom in a hierarchal "chain-of-command." Decisions are made at the top, and orders are issued, followed by a virtual domino effect of obedience and conformity. The recognition of (and resignation to) this piece of social reality is crucial in accepting all other facets of consumer philosophy. In fact, this is at the heart of "manufacturing consent."

The U.S. Department of Education has responsibility over most educational activities in the country. These responsibilities pass down the bureaucratic structure to state levels, to municipalities, to school districts, and finally to schools. Against this backdrop, the personal identities of children as young as five or six years old are immediately subsumed into the institutional identity of "student," which carries with it certain responsibilities, but no authority. Indeed, students are at the bottom of the educational power structure. Therefore, they learn not only reading and writing, but also respect for authority and how to obey orders. Teachers teach; students learn and obey. Even more important, students learn to regard formal authority as *ubiquitous*—as indeed it usually will be for the next 50 or 60 years of their lives.

There is a strong aura of *conditioning* to this process. In fact, the term "socialization" refers specifically to the process of social and cultural indoctrination.

From a broad, over-all perspective, we see that the school systems inside the U.S. and other "developed" countries are designed to produce salaried workers and consumers. This view is not surprising in cultures based on consumerism and corporatism. What is surprising is how deeply ingrained these concepts become within the hearts and minds of citizens, so much so that it's hard for people to imagine alternative lifestyles.

We have discovered that a great number of college students attended the university "to get a good job." A good job was most often defined by money and, much less often, love for the subject. Very few questioned the existence of the university or its standard "liberal arts" curricula or the desire for a "good job." These students had been groomed their entire lives to prepare for entry into "work," and they rarely thought twice about it, as if this particular life-track was the only one available (or visible). In fact, the responses were strikingly similar for children in the sixth grade: "Get a good job" and "Make a lot of money." Of course, there were exceptional students who regarded their education as an exercise in enlightenment and self-fulfillment rather than preparation for "work."

What can we deduce from these responses? Is it possible the creation of great wealth and huge corporations pushed the U.S. educational process in this direction (Mayer, 2016)? We notice that several well-known universities were founded and funded in the nineteenth century by wealthy "captains of industry." Most assuredly these "captains" influenced the character of the administrative structure and the choice of curricula (Teachout, 2016).

Also, taking into account the social milieu, these changes in U.S. education occurred during a period of mass migration into the United States, with hundreds of thousands of immigrants looking for a place to live, something to eat, a job. A series of social movements and shifts in relations of power came together and set the Cultural Model on the road to where it is now—producing salaried workers and consumers.

By taking education out of the intimate arena of family and local control, the government created conditions that treated students as *individuals* rather than familiar members of the community. This is the usual nature of human-created formal institutions; they typically operate on a system of *positions*, rather than personalities. The word "student" is synonymous with "individual"; that is, it carries a completely anonymous quality (as does "consumer" or "citizen").

No other element of the school experience reinforces this emphasis on individuality more than the atmosphere of *competition*. The grading system used by most schools promotes competition by approval of "good" grades and disapproval of "bad" grades, or by "passing" and "failing." At home also, students are often rewarded or punished according to their grades. There is a general belief that "bad" students become the salaried workers making an hourly wage, while the "good" students will eventually work in offices (and wear suits?) and receive their salaries by the week or month.

Since most schools use a "curve" grading system, students know their grades are determined by their progress in relation to their classmates; thus, the social "field" that develops among students becomes more adversarial than cooperative. There are only a few "A's" and "B's," quite a few "C's and only a few "D's" and "F's." In these "reward opportunities," students are presented with a range of quality. "A's" are of superior quality, scarce, and supposedly go only to those most worthy or of superior ability. No one wants to fail, all hope to pass, but an "A" is hard to earn.

Young children in school learn to strive for quality rewards and avoid "mediocrity" or "failure." This pattern of behavior is immensely important because it is especially suited to salaried employment and consumption of goods and services. Most citizens want to "move up the ladder of success" and "make something of themselves." They accumulate valuable things for convenience and comfort, to augment their personal and social identities, and to demonstrate their level of "success."

Since human children have learned that their possessions reflect directly on their identity, they are driven to accumulate quality things—like "good grades" or "awards." Later in life, after they've "graduated," most of their waking hours will be dedicated to working and consuming. Also, of course, they'll be in a competition of consumption with their neighbors and co-workers.

We want to stress that this individual, competitive philosophy is not a singular lesson taught by nature; it is simply a component of the Cultural Model. Humans regard it as a "reality" that seems always to have existed and always will. But it is merely a state of mind—that is, a forced or *chosen* philosophy—and not an inherent condition of the social universe.

Students of a certain age share the same classroom (and occasionally wear the same uniform). Behind the identical formal identities are peculiar personalities with various mental capacities and physical abilities. However, these personal qualities are ostensibly not considered while evaluating the "student." School officials claim that "fairness" demands that all students be judged according to their performance in relation to their classmates.

Our observations indicate that a myriad of social and cultural factors come into play influencing a child's performance at school. Also, some humans are simply faster, smarter, or bigger than others. Nonetheless, the formal procedures of school posit a "level playing field" (a competitive metaphor) for all students.

Within such a social context, we notice a schizophrenic process—although the children are part of a group of students, they are evaluated as individuals. This is when a social disconnect occurs, triggering the beginning of isolation and anomie. It is the strange condition of living within a community, yet remaining an individual apart. Feelings of anomie and powerlessness may influence an individual's mental and emotional health, and performance at school or job.

This individual/competitive philosophy is a central motivating factor in the consumption and accumulation of things. When the humans see themselves as anonymous individuals within a sea of anonymous strangers, expression of personal identity becomes important. They are encouraged to "stand out from the crowd" and to "make their mark on the world," to "be themselves." They have learned to express their personal peculiarities with their "look" and the things they attach to their person, including "consumer goods."

We observed customers roaming through an automobile sales center. Although most had settled on a price limit and expressed concern about gas mileage, the majority of their comments were of a personal nature: "That's my favorite color," or "I'm too hip for that piece of crap," or "This one's like me—fast, strong, and sexy." Corporate marketing departments know these psychic, "ingrained" interests, and construct promotional campaigns targeted on the desire to constantly "express" one's self.

One more aspect of this individuality needs to be mentioned. A country full of individuals is substantially different politically than a country full of highly integrated communities. Communities can feel their power in numbers, but individuals are alone and usually powerless. Obviously, this weaker condition makes it difficult for humans to come together in common cause. Conversely, it makes it easier for law enforcement agencies to maintain control with a minimum of force. However, there are exceptions, when one person has come to symbolize an entire nation or movement; such as Mahatma Gandhi, Dalai Lama, Nelson Mandela, or Sister Teresa. These leaders initially were labeled as deviants, but became seen as political deviants or "heroes"—those who channeled the peoples' power and changed history.

Patriotism is also taught in schools, usually in the form of "history." In the U.S. children are taught stories that illustrate the uniqueness and "goodness" of the "founding fathers" of the country. For example, there is a story about George Washington admitting to chopping down a cherry tree, demonstrating that he could not tell a lie. There is the brave ride of Paul Revere in the nighttime, stories of Ben Franklin's genius, Thomas Paine's intellect, and Thomas Jefferson's political purity. These great historical personages loom large in the minds of U.S. school children, sort of like political deities. In addition, the history books reveal their patriarchal character by mentioning only a few women as participating in the Revolution—Betsy Ross, Nancy Hart, and Abigail Adams — and they were usually depicted as cooking or sewing or nursing.

U.S. students pledge allegiance to the United States and there are American flags in most classrooms. Most U.S. children believe they live in the best, richest, most powerful country in the world. How could they know any different?

Young children absorb information quickly and usually do not question the accuracy or source. They are highly observant and curious about the world around them, and, as they explore, they look to adults—parents, teachers and other authority figures—to keep them safe and give them good directions. Growing up within the U.S. Cultural Model, and isolated for the most part from other cultures, children are exposed to the dominant cultural point of view. The information children receive shapes their attitudes and values regarding their country and the rest of the world.

The educational experience is an important process of becoming a "citizen." Here again, the term "citizen" carries an anonymous quality, until it is qualified with the word "American," or "Mexican," or any other nationality. Most humans are citizens of a particular nation living in a multi-national world, but each nationality regards the world through the peculiar prism of their own Cultural Model.

There is the danger that an overabundance of patriotism can lead to an ethnocentric view of the world. If one lives in the best, richest, and most powerful country on Earth, the rest of the world might become viewed as secondhand, or worse.

Here we find a curious development: The aforementioned philosophy of individuals in competition is carried up to the level of whole societies. Americans and other nationalities usually act as if they're alone in the world and must compete with other nations for scarce resources, "markets" and consumption. An adversarial relationship develops as each nation pursues its own agenda, making alliances, breaking alliances, and confronting the opposition (which doesn't bode well in a world loaded with nuclear weapons).

Finally, in any discussion of education, it's necessary to remember the teachers. How they present themselves and the information they impart can have a profound impact on young children. Although a teacher's role is arguably the most important in the society, they are near the bottom of the educational power structure, and some of the poorest paid workers in the country. Even stranger is comparing the salaries of top athletic personnel to salaries of teachers and professors, especially at the big universities. Sometimes the imbalances are huge, with some athletic coaches earning millions of dollars annually. These imbalances illustrate an important point, which we will touch on later; teachers impart knowledge, while many football coaches enhance the university's *image*.

Religion is also entwined with education. In Catholic grade schools in the United States, and in some public schools, it is understood that "God" is, for the most part, a Christian American God. (In Iranian schools, the children understand that "God" is Allah and Mohammed was His Prophet.) We examined "catechisms" (written pamphlets) from the 1950s distributed to U.S. Catholic schools and designed to instruct students in the Catholic faith. Church and school officials took the opportunity to include political propaganda in the catechism. In one of these booklets we saw a cartoon supposedly depicting a classroom in the Soviet Union, showing children sitting at their desks with looks of horror on their faces, while the teacher—a tall, angular figure with an angry face—pointed a long, crooked finger at the blackboard, which said this: There is no God! Apparently, this was supposed to demonstrate the "godless" quality of "communism" to American children.

As a subject of education, "religion" is a concept with millions of meanings. Most humans have some personal idea about the workings of the universe and the meaning of the birth-life-death cycle. However, the term "religion" refers more to an organized spiritual philosophy and includes all spiritual groupings—from the Indians in the Amazon rainforest to the Catholics in Rome.

The Indian religions are likely to be highly localized, verbal, rooted in nature, and usually passed on to children through oral tradition. However, the Catholics, Protestants, Islamists, Jews, and other "mainstream" religions involve gigantic institutions with elaborate rituals, mountains of written doctrine, their own special schools and seminaries, and minutiae of spiritual necessities and requirements. They are also centralized power structures and, as such, obey the laws of all formal institutions, despite the differences in their "credos." Their political power is considerable, and they have an impact on global events, as well as the personal lives of believers and non-believers.

Religious education occurs on many levels—sometimes in the formal school classroom, especially in private religious schools—but also learned through every-day social interaction and even ethnic heritage. We witnessed a "baptism" (initiation ceremony) in a Catholic Church. The initiate was only six months old. Children so young have no idea what's happening, but over time religion often becomes part of the child's personal identity. They'll participate in solemn rituals of passage and instruction until they're finally considered a full member of the "congregation." Within the U.S. Cultural Model, the most prevalent religion is Christianity, and most children born in the U.S. will be instructed in the Christian religion. (However, this Christianity is also split up into many different "sects"—for example, Baptists, Methodists, Seventh Day Adventists, Evangelicals and others—each with their own interpretations of the Bible.)

The Christian religion arrived on American soil with the first wave of European settlers. Before this, American Indians held a variety of spiritual beliefs. Although each indigenous community practiced its own sacred ceremonies and cared for sacred places, religious experiences were generally grounded in nature and natural events, and some shared among diverse first nations. The creation stories of many indigenous communities shared similar elements: The First People emerged from the Earth, and the Earth nourished the People, giving them life and meaning and a collective identity. Among the Indians, religious experience is a way of life, deeply connected to the lessons learned from nature.

Christianity, on the other hand, is based on something that occurred centuries ago in a land somewhere far from America, and yet it is supposed to apply to every human being on Earth at all times, including the Indians who had not heard of it. Christianity exists as a series of formal doctrines written inside a book (as do most other mainstream religions). Its central tenets are based on authority, time, and history, rather than collectivity, nature, and experience.

Education in each country tends to focus on the home culture and is infused with nationalist feelings and attitudes

(Adamson, Åstrand, and Darling-Hammond, 2016). This "isolation" and lack of information about foreign cultures can lead to ethnocentrism, and the same is true with spiritual beliefs. The Christian religion permeates the U.S. Cultural Model and most European cultures. In the U.S. there is even a strong feeling that God approves of America and that God is on America's side. "God Bless America" is a popular song and U.S. currency carries the words "In God We Trust." (The phrase first appeared on U.S. coins in the middle 1800s, near the end of the Civil War. It was added to the paper currency in the 1950s after the Second World War.)

Here is a coincidence of powerful forces, a combination of national identity with a deity, both of which are incorporated into a person's identity—they are Americans; they are Christians. When humans claim a thing or an idea as "mine," they have a reflection of "self-feeling" toward that thing or idea. For example, if someone insults the United States or Christianity, Americans are likely to take the insult personally, as if it was directed at their person—and, in a way, it is. We point out that the same process is at work in other "faiths"; for example, many Muslims are easily offended by Western depictions of Muhammad.

This social psychological process sets up "boundaries" around personal identities—limits to the beliefs and values people claim. Christianity is *here* and in their hearts, while Islam is *over there* and strange and possibly heretic. And Islam regards Christianity with a similar measure of hesitancy and caution, and it's easy to understand why: These two religions share centuries of bloody, contentious history, not only with each other, but with other "heresies."

These internal boundaries act not only to define each human's identity, but also as mental prisms through which they interpret social reality. However, it also works the other way; the boundaries that keep them in will keep others out. If they claim to be a Muslim or Christian, then they must ignore or criticize other religious beliefs. At best, other religions are heretic; at worst, they're the work of the "devil." The mental boundaries act as indicators to distinguish "us" from "them."

In this way humans become prisoners of their own Cultural Model; by learning to live a certain way and believe particular ideas, they exclude all or most other ways and ideas. This process is called *socialization*—when the surrounding social context imparts its beliefs and customs on the next generation. These boundaries also separate political deviants who often challenge the status quo for a higher moral good versus deviants who primarily act for selfish reasons.

With so many different cultures replicating themselves, we have a partial explanation for why Earthlings are so different from each other. They do not yet see themselves primarily as *human*, but rather as Russian, Chinese, or American. Also, within each culture there are large and small groups of identities, all of which work to create millions of social realities that coalesce into a particular culture.

Even more curious is that cultural animosities—conflicts among different nationalities or ethnic groups—also replicate themselves over the years and centuries. There are cultural rivalries on Earth that go back hundreds of years, long after the principle "causes" have been forgotten. Such cultural animosities can be the result of a single incident and carried forward through generations. In the 1930s when Japan invaded China, Japanese troops committed atrocious crimes, especially in Nanking. Japan has not apologized formally for these war crimes, and China has not forgiven Japan. Now, approximately 70 years later, this event still colors relations between the two countries. Cultural grievances and animosities are imparted to the next generation, even when the principle actors are long gone.

The contrary process can also happen, when organizations and movements emerge together under "friendly" terms, only to turn against each other. For example, three of Earth's largest religions—Christianity, Judaism, and Islam — descended from the same patriarch, Abraham, but fell out with each other over points of political and economic interests, and doctrine. Now, as gigantic organizations, they operate more as enemies than as close cousins.

This same transference of grievance also occurs within cultures along ethnic lines. For example, countries that practiced slavery hundreds of years ago are still plagued with the racist attitudes and behaviors that characterized the slave trade.

Education inside most technologically developed countries is a consumption activity. Most parents can afford most of the costs related to public grade schools and high schools. Also, in most "developed" countries, attending primary school is a legal obligation, and the state will usually subsidize the costs to lower-income families.

Nevertheless, knowledge is a commodity for sale, especially "higher education," and students are often referred to as "consumers of education." In this commodity transaction, schools provide knowledge and students pay for it. The costs in the United States of primary, secondary, and college education range from nearly "free" public schools to extremely expensive private schools.

The price of knowledge is considerably more expensive in "higher education." The average tuition at colleges and universities in the United States has increased every year over the last 30 years. At the same time, the medium family income remained fairly dormant and, according to the latest census, has decreased in the last few years. This report also means that higher education has become less accessible to a larger part of the population. This process might be considered a sort of "economic discrimination."

Consumption and use of education, or knowledge, is a slightly different consumer activity from our previous examples. There are producers—colleges and universities—and there are consumers—students—but the product is intellectual and leaves behind little or no "trash" of the material type. (However, some of the "intellectual" work we've uncovered may be regarded as "trash.")

Higher education is usually not an end in itself, but rather preparation for one's chosen "profession." We've seen several studies that confirm a college or university degree enhances one's chances of securing a higher income "job." Part of this is due to the changes in types of employment in the United States; the manufacturing and assembly industries have given way to technical and technology-related industries, most of which require some education beyond high school.

Inside most developed countries, where most things and people are judged on image and status, the educational system operates on the same social wavelength. For example, we discovered a huge difference in the tradition and prestige of *Harvard Business School* in Cambridge, Massachusetts, in comparison with *Cameron State Junior Agricultural College* in Lawton, Oklahoma.

In fact, this status ranking of schools has been the subject of study by former U.S. Secretary of Education William Bennett and his colleague David Wilezol (2013). They calculated what they called "return on investment" at 3500 colleges and universities in the United States. They included tuition costs for residents and non-residents, room and board, and books, and compared these costs to the average expected starting salary for a college graduate. Also, they took into account the enormous student loan debt in the United States—at over one trillion dollars. (In fact, student debt is the second biggest U.S. household debt, after mortgages.)

According to Bennett and Wilezol, only 150 institutions of higher education appeared worth the cost of the diploma, at least in regards to starting salaries and expected future earnings. Further, this "worth" is not a component of the curricula or of the knowledge received; rather it is related to *where* one learns the knowledge. The status and prestige of the school determines the life tracks of thousands of college students. To get a flavor of this ranking process, here are the top ten schools in their list of "return on investment":

1. Harvey Mudd College
2. California Institute of Technology
3. Massachusetts Institute of Technology (MIT)
4. Stanford University
5. Princeton University
6. Harvard University
7. Dartmouth College
8. Duke University
9. University of Pennsylvania
10. University of Notre Dame

We have engaged in a short debate about what this might mean. First, we agree that "knowledge" is the same everywhere. The laws of physics, mathematics, and chemistry are the same on Earth as on our world. Further, we agree that these bodies of knowledge carry no particular ranking or value—they are simply numeric/symbolic reflections of observable physical reality.

It was suggested that perhaps some schools teach the knowledge better. This would indicate higher quality, and thus a higher cost. We agreed this is a possibility, but the quality is in the teaching, not the knowledge. Therefore, the best schools are the ones with high quality teachers.

However, upon further investigation, we found little evidence of wide differences in teaching quality—at least not enough to justify the higher "returns on investment." There were exceptions up and down, but generally the quality level of instruction across the United States remained constant. We conclude that Bennett's claim must be accurate; in most cases, *the image of a school is worth more than the education.* (However, we also discovered that exceptional students from any school eventually excelled at their professions.) Related to this process is that high status schools tend to attract students of high social position, offering opportunities to forge personal alliances and contacts among the economic elite—the infamous "Skull and Bones" club at Yale is a prime example.

For high school graduates thinking about attending college, this "prestige" ranking is related directly to levels of income. Generally, if they have no chance at a scholarship, they may attend the college or university they (and their family or guardians) can afford. The costs of this education must fall within their budget, their level of consumption, or they can take out a student loan. This forces students to "shop" for an education. Plus, they focus more on costs and "return investments" than on the process of accumulating knowledge. In fact, it is common to find internet social networks advertising "the best college degrees that deliver the most income."

Student loan programs help students pay for college, but also load them heavily with debt. In 2013, about two thirds of U.S. college graduates had some sort of debt. The average student borrower graduates with a debt of $29,600. Over several years, with interest added, this debt is likely to be $40,000. One in ten graduates will accumulate more than $50,000, while about 1 percent of graduates will have a debt of $100,000 or more.

These students have essentially mortgaged their near future by betting on diplomas that will lead to higher earnings. Generally, this is true, but not always, as the above ranking of "prestige colleges" demonstrates. Further, the pressure of repaying these loans—under the awful threat of "bad credit rating"—does not allow graduates the luxury to pick and choose jobs. In this sense, with several years of payments due, graduates are held hostage to their jobs, like it or not. Moreover, the over-all economy suffers eventually because these new consumers forego the purchase of homes and "big-ticket" consumer goods until the loans are repaid.

If one overcomes the difficulties of access to higher education, the graduate enters a "workforce" that is still stagnant or even contracting from the most recent "recession." More than 3.5 million Americans work at or below the minimum wage, up more than 50 percent from a decade ago, and government data show that the numbers of minimum wage workers have increased even among those with college and advanced degrees. The number of college graduates working minimum wage jobs is nearly *71 percent* higher than it was a decade ago, according to the Bureau of Labor Statistics.

If people can't afford higher education, they seem forced to delay or give up ambitions of attending college. This delay or denial is a direct result of one's position within the economic structure; the higher the family income, the greater the access to college; the lower the income, the less the access.

The community-level reality of this condition is measured in underemployment, lost opportunities, frustration, and heartbreak. The inequality of access means that millions of young people are denied a higher education, not because of ability or ambition, but because *inequality is an inherent component of the social structure.*

These are strange conditions. The U.S. culture promotes unlimited consumerism and the accumulation of things, but then limits the opportunities to participate. Consumers are required to establish a good line of credit, pay with credit cards, arrange title loans, or take out a mortgage, and this often causes insecurity about meeting the monthly bills. On the other hand, we noticed that limiting the opportunities ensures a constantly insecure, docile, and plentiful workforce.

Students are treated as "consumers" and "higher education" is a precious commodity, making access to colleges and universities troublesome for some citizens. However, we have noticed that colleges and universities permit nearly unlimited access to private companies.

Corporate involvement in U.S. universities increased substantially after the Bayh-Dole Act of 1980, and later amendments. This legislation was intended to clarify and standardize patent rights regarding government-funded research. The act also made an effort to improve and increase agricultural output and technical invention by encouraging patent agreements and licensing rights between universities and private companies. Since then, research activity between universities and the private sector has evolved into a close, lucrative cooperation. For example, from 1985 to 2005, private industry funding of university research increased by *250 percent*, from $950 million to $2.4 billion, according to the American Association for the Advancement of Science. In the years since, corporate funding has continued to increase.

Corporations give "grants" or "endowments" to universities in exchange for special privileges—such as "locking-in" licensing and patent agreements, the right to name buildings or professorships, participate in basic research, and turn lab innovations into commercial applications.

The U.S. agribusiness giant Monsanto has "invested" heavily in universities and is a clear example of corporate involvement in U.S. higher education. Here are only some of its involvements in major universities: Monsanto has a professorship in its name at the University of Florida, for which it paid $600,000. In 2010 Monsanto donated $500,000 for a faculty chair in soybean breeding at Iowa State University and pledged another $1 million, which ensured naming rights to the Monsanto Student Services Wing in the main agriculture building. Monsanto gave $2.5 million to Texas A&M to endow the Monsanto chairpersonship in plant breeding. University of Missouri houses a Monsanto Auditorium. Monsanto gave $200,000 to the college of agriculture at the University of Illinois to establish the Monsanto Multi-Media Executive Studio.

Monsanto protects its new breed of genetically modified (GMO) seeds—created with the help of university scientists—with binding patents that include a clause prohibiting any outside agency from analyzing Monsanto seeds without permission from Monsanto. Aside from making it impossible for objective scientific analysis, this maneuver defeats the whole purpose of precise scientific research and the pursuit of knowledge—not to mention a potential danger to consumers and the environment.

GMO foods are not natural; they are *modified*. Plant researchers found a way to "knockdown" specific genes that trigger particular reactions—for example, resistance to certain insects or fungus. For example, a GMO plant will no longer help in the survival of harmful microbes—those particular genes are knocked down—so the microbes die off and the modified plant survives.

A GMO plant may look and taste the same as a natural plant, but some microbes are essential to particular ecosystems, helping to break down the sun's energy stored in plants and animals. Also, some plants may require periodic visits by their predators. For example, the grasses of the Great Plains had a special growth rate—whenever under "stress" the plant would grow quickly and strongly. The "stress" exerted on these grasses were millions of grazing buffalo eating at the grasses. This created a symbiotic relationship; the grasses needed the buffalo and the buffalo needed the grasses (O'Brien, 2002). Also, wolves, grizzly bears, and coyotes preyed on the buffalo, extending the food chain. This example demonstrates the fine balance in natural systems, including the importance of predators, but this balance may be at danger from introducing "modified" plants.

Monsanto claims that the only question about the difference between GMO crops and natural crops should be addressed to the *outcome*—the produce. This argument is called "substantially equivalent," which means that each plant's *produce* is virtually the same. Their website (www.monsanto.com: p. 9) says this: "So long as the introduced protein is determined to be safe, food from GM crops determined to be substantially equivalent is not expected to pose any health risks."

This argument is based in part on the belief that genetic material from food is not absorbed into the human body. However, Chinese scientists at Nanjing University reported discovery of the ribonucleic acid (RNA) of rice inside human cells. This rice genetic material connects with receptors in human liver cells and impacts the absorption of cholesterol from the blood. This finding strongly suggests that plant genes can transfer to the humans who eat them and that those genes have an impact on the biology of human bodies. These findings open up a whole new line of inquiry regarding GMO food crops.

Most GMO foods are not labeled as such. Most cooking oils, corn, cereals, and sodas contain GMOs, especially high fructose corn syrup, which is used in thousands of products, mostly as a sweetener. GMOs are not regulated by the government and do not need advisory labels. At this time food advocates in several states are pressuring legislatures to force labeling of GMOs, while Monsanto and other agri-corporations fight these labeling efforts by lobbying lawmakers and making "donations."

Other agri-business giants are also active in academia; Kraft Foods donated $1 million to the University of Illinois for a professorship in its name in the school of nutrition.

The food science department at Purdue University received almost 40 percent of its research grants from private corporations, including Nestlé and PepsiCo.

Technology and nanotechnology corporations are also active in university research. In 2005 Google, Microsoft, and Sun Microsystems agreed to donate a five-year grant of $7.5 million to fund research at the Reliable, Adaptive, and Distributed Systems Laboratory at UC Berkeley. In 2006 the RAD lab received additional funding from other technology companies, including Hewlett-Packard, IBM, and Oracle. The funding supports the research and pays for stipends and salaries. In return, the corporations lock-in licensing rights for commercial markets.

University professors are often hired as "consultants" by private corporations and paid accordingly. For example, even 10 years ago it was evident that nearly one-third of land-grant agricultural scientists also worked for private industry. Nine years later that percentage is higher, including in the technology industry. This practice also tends to influence attitudes toward corporate sponsors, because the salaries and grants are highly appreciated. In any case, many professors or "scientists" also grew up with the consumerist philosophy and see little wrong with augmenting their incomes through close association with private companies, or, in some cases, lend their names to "studies" that support corporate claims, in spite of contrary evidence.

In the social sciences we see consumerist influences on the attitudes of sociologists. In our introduction we noted the cultural biases present among sociologists, including attitudes and values related to their university experience. In this regard, we discovered a perspective called the sociology of sociology.

Alvin Gouldner, a sociologist, describes the selective process of grants for research and "study," and how those grants are granted. He demonstrates how dominant cultural ideas filter into academia from institutional and corporate sponsors. The result is the shaping of hearts and minds into particular directions.

Gouldner (1970) puts it this way:

> The most fundamental control device of any stable social system is not its use of crude force, or even of other, nonviolent forms of punishment, but its continuing distribution of mundane rewards. It is not simply power that elites seek and use, but an authority that is rooted in the readiness of others to credit its good intentions, to cease contention when it has rendered its decision, to accept its conception of social reality, and to reject alternatives at variance with the status quo. The most effective strategy to induce such conformity is to make it worthwhile. What elites prefer is not craven expedience, but pious opportunism…those who supply the greatest resources for the institutional development of sociology are precisely those who most distort its quest for knowledge. (p. 219)

This process describes a clear reward and punishment system designed to ensure that scientists with the proper attitudes advance, while those who are suspect or uncooperative are ignored. The passage upward is guarded by "gatekeepers" with the authority to admit or deny entrance into higher levels of consumption and power. In this sense, "upward mobility" is an exercise in conformity.

Another sociologist, Peter Berger (2011), addresses this problem in *Invitation to Sociology*: "The sociologist will normally have many values as a citizen, a private person, a member of a religious group, or an adherent of some other association of people. But within his activities as a sociologist there is one fundamental value only—that of scientific integrity… [Sociology] strives to be an act of pure perception, as pure as humanly limited means allow. Although 'objectivity' is always the goal, it is rarely achieved" (p. 4).

There is an uncertainty principle involved; subjective perceptions cannot arrive at a completely objective analysis. From a reductionist perspective, each person's history is unique, and it's a person's history that determines present perspective. In fact, in full recognition of our own cultural biases—which must be considerable because we're *aliens*—this report will include thousands of visual/audio recordings of human interactions from all over Earth, allowing for verification.

Motives (intentions in law) are also relevant to the profession of sociology, as they are to all professions, and motives are generally embedded in our personal identity. For example, most academic institutions and universities demand a certain amount of tangible "products" from their professors—books and articles—especially junior professors hoping for tenure. In this case, research and study can become a means to enhance and maintain one's career, even though most "studies" might focus on minor or abstruse subjects.

Some sociologists and psychologists are in the employ of corporations and the government, using social theory to promote private interests and government policy. However, this work involves more of an application of theory, rather than pure research.

Finally, there is the motive of joy and passion in discovery and understanding, especially when these discoveries transform the obvious into the wondrous. Apart from cultural biases, sociology has the power to redefine existing social dynamics and illuminate the shadowy corners of everyday life. Peter Berger again: "There is another excitement of discovery beckoning [the sociologist's] investigations. It is not the excitement of coming upon the totally unfamiliar, but rather the excitement of finding the familiar becoming transformed in its meaning. The fascination of sociology lies in the fact that its perspective makes us see in a new light the very world in which we have lived all our lives" (p. 69).

As state and federal assistance to universities continues to shrink, private enterprise steps into the vacuum. This is important to highlight because this growing dependence on corporate funding is skewing the nature and direction of university scientific research. The emphasis now is on short-term commercial applications, rather than pure research on the frontiers of knowledge. It even influences the very structure and "social field" of academia by discouraging research that might challenge the claims of corporate donors, or upset grant-hungry administrators who confer tenure on young professors. In the case of food science, for example, university-corporate research tends to reinforce the industrial model and focuses on commodity crops, such as soy beans and corn, instead of fruits and vegetables or sustainable production techniques. Also, water science appears to be following in a similar direction, and water is a vital component of life.

It is worth reflecting on the original human idea of "university" and its applications in ancient times. Back then, "education" meant a thorough grounding in all the sciences, including ethics, philosophy, and citizenship. Education meant learning and expanding the frontiers of knowledge, perfecting political philosophy, and developing systems of ethical or "right" behavior—humans learning to live with each other.

In contrast, the modern human university education is focused on "work," "future earnings," and "consumption" with little emphasis on self-fulfillment, engaged citizenship, or ethical behavior (Schaeffer, 2016). It is our conclusion that with an educational system dedicated primarily to work and consumption, human society in general suffers from a loss of vitality, creativity, and cohesion.

CHAPTER 3: DRUGS

Aside from consumption of goods and services and education, humans consume great quantities of drugs, which also impacts directly on the socio-economic structure. Human consumption of "mind-altering" substances is as old as recorded history. Drug use is a global phenomenon, and drugs are grown and produced all over the world. Humans use drugs in a vast array of social situations; for example, in religious ceremonies, sexual enhancement, mind expansion, interrogation, social control, or recreation.

However, present-day drug consumption is problematic in that humans have divided drugs into two general categories—legal and illegal. Some drugs, such as medical prescriptions, alcohol and, in a few cases, marijuana, are legal to purchase and consume. Most other drugs have been defined as illegal, and vast law enforcement bureaucracies have been created to combat trafficking in illegal drugs. Although most drugs can produce powerful physical effects, especially if abused, it is not clear why some drugs are legal and others are not.

For generations, indigenous populations around the world used drugs—most often hallucinogens—during sacred ceremonies and special occasions. When Europeans arrived on American shores they brought a long history of drug use, usually alcohol.

For centuries, alcohol was legal in the United States until the early part of last century when several powerful social movements came together and forced the U.S. Congress to define alcohol as illegal. However, this "Prohibition" of alcohol only highlighted the depth of U.S. cultural tradition in con-suming it—at least three fourths of the country engaged regu-larly in criminal behavior.

Finally, after much violence committed against people and property and the illicit enrichment of thousands of citizens, Prohibition was repealed. This powerful and painful national experience confirmed the following economic reality; if there is a demand—whether for toothbrushes, gin, or cocaine—some-one will supply the product. This market process is at the heart of entrepreneurship.

Alcohol is now legal again in the United States and is by far the most often consumed drug. There is also a market for illegal drugs, and typically has been. The U.S. government has conducted "drug wars" in the past, usually as a means of social control—and this reveals a clue as to how drugs become illegal. For example, the illegalization of smoking opium in the 19th century was explicitly enacted to control the grow-ing Chinese population along the West Coast. (Ironically, the Chinese were first lured to work on West Coast railroads with promises to supply opium.) Other governments have also ma-nipulated the drug trade as a political tool, most notoriously the British, when they controlled large parts of China by ap-plying the "stoned" fist of opium. Also, the present thriving heroin industry is dependent on Afghanistan poppy fields, which are clearly within reach of U.S. and Afghan authorities. Yet, according to the United Nations, Afghanistan provides 90% of the world's poppy crop. In Vietnam U.S. person-nel—principally "rogue" agents of the CIA—ran marijuana and heroin from Southeast Asia to the U.S., sometimes using their own airline, "Air America."

U.S. history books rarely note the political manipulation of opiates and other drugs. The use of opiates in early U.S. his-tory was legal, common, and widespread; they were sold usu-ally as bottled "patent medicines," many of which contained opium. Although the physical/chemical reactions of opium on the human body were largely unknown at the time, there was no doubt its narcotic effects alleviated pain and uncomfortable symptoms. (In fact, hawkers of bottled "miracle water" claimed to cure almost any disease or ailment.)

In the 1800s, a German chemist created a derivative from opium called "morphium." This discovery initiated a shift from pure opium as a folk medicine to a complex technology of other derivatives such as codeine, dionin, and heroin.

The opiate derivatives became popularly prescribed for all sorts of ailments. One doctor, for example, reported that opium could be used for relief of pain in venereal disease, cancer, nervous headaches, palpitations, vomiting, dysentery, and diarrhea. Morphine was believed to benefit anemia, angina, asthma, bronchitis, cardiac diseases, cholera, convulsions, delirium tremens, diabetes, epilepsy, insanity, insomnia, nymphomania, pneumonia, shock, and vomiting during pregnancy.

Since early medical remedies were directed at symptoms rather than cures, a drug that apparently suited such a range of medical situations became widely administered and enthusiastically taken. The high potency and addictive qualities of these medicines resulted in an increase in addiction—a higher per capita addiction rate than today. However, the addiction did not carry a particularly odious connotation, and addicts were not stigmatized socially. In the absence of scientific knowledge about the true effects of opium, it was assumed that addiction was related to some weakness or defect in personal character, or a "side-effect" of the drug, or even an unrelated condition. Nevertheless, addiction did not arouse a sense of stigma or outrage. Moreover, the drugs were plentiful and cheap, and addicts did not have to resort to drastic means to obtain them.

We traced the changing definition of opium use in the United States to a law enacted in San Francisco in 1875, which prohibited the smoking of opium. This "law" was in response to several social forces reacting to the presence of Chinese immigrants. Economic depression, the rise of labor unions, and high unemployment coalesced into a focus on Chinese workers, especially after the transcontinental railroad had been finished. The surplus Chinese workforce became rivals in the search for employment. Chinese traditional use of opium provided the perfect political and economic tool.

The earliest drug laws were not simply motivated by the potential harmfulness of the drug or any commitment to social welfare, but by government and business demands for economic stability and political control. The application of a negative label to Chinese opium smokers was a precursor of modern attitudes about opiates.

In the early part of last century, during the movement to rationalize the law, the federal government consolidated control and power over several American institutions, including education, law, corporations, medical practice, and importation and regulation of "controlled substances." The Harrison Act of 1914 declared that opiates sold on the streets and consumed for nonmedical purposes were illegal. Drug abuse and addiction were no longer regarded as medical conditions, but as criminal activity. On the other hand, opiates sold for medical purposes by "medical professionals" were legal.

These definitions have led to unintended consequences; by declaring certain drugs "illegal," an underground market is automatically created—leading to the growth of a giant clandestine drug industry and all the corruption and violence it breeds.

The Harrison Act was the result of several social forces of varied interests coalescing around the issue of opium and manipulating the regulations and conditions of its sale and consumption. These regulations had little to do with the properties of the drug and more to do with consumption, politics, bureaucracy, and corporatization. In this sense, the regulation of drugs, legal or illegal, follows the same model as the consumption of everything else—in the interests of private profit.

From our perspective, it's hard to see the "crime" in the consumption of any drug, since it is usually a voluntary activity. If the drug is dangerous or fatal for the person, then why isn't the crime for those who produce and sell it, rather than the consumer? However, if the effect of the drug produces relief or a harmless "high" and has a negligible or benign effect on social relations, then what type of crime is it?

Apparently, the essence of the crime is not found in the act of production and consumption, since there appear to be no "victims," but only because the *written legal code* says it's a crime. Of course, this seems absurd and irrational. We conclude that the primary reason such a legal code exists is because it serves some political or private interest.

In spite of the new laws, illegal drug consumption still continued—cocaine, heroin, and marijuana—but it was usually confined to subcultures. In the forties and fifties, illegal drug use was common within the "beatnik" and jazz subculture, but did not penetrate significantly into the general population. However, the 1960s experienced a huge increase in consumption of illegal drugs—in both the United States and Europe—and this increase ostensibly led to the huge "drug problem" presently menacing the populations of several countries.

U.S. involvement in Vietnam helped expand the explosion of "illegal" drug use in the sixties and seventies. Most U.S. military personnel were sent to Vietnam straight out of high school—the average age was 19—and served a tour of one year. These young men and women were sent thousands of miles from home, inside a strange culture, and with people trying to kill each other. These conditions, plus the easy availability of drugs, led to widespread drug use among the U.S. military, mostly marijuana, but also heroin and opium. (In

1967 in Vietnam a pack of 20 high-grade marijuana cigarettes cost one dollar.) Millions of soldiers from all over the United States went to Vietnam, got stoned, came home, and created a *market*.

The modern day illegal drug trade began as a series of informal enterprises within the "hippie" subculture. During the early days of mass drug use, we saw references to the sale of "lids" of marijuana, but we can't find a definition for this term. (We think it means a measurement, perhaps "one ounce.") Illegal drug use slowly expanded into the general population, and eventually the drug trade grew into the giant international, multibillion-dollar business it is today. According to a relatively new U.N. study, after oil and arms, illegal drugs are the most traded commodity in the world, with global profits around 400 billion dollars a year. Moreover, the world's governments spend billions of dollars on anti-drug activities, in addition to spending millions to incarcerate people charged with "drug crimes."

To fight this most recent war on drugs, the U.S. government created a new federal bureaucracy, the Drug Enforcement Administration (DEA) and gave it a yearly budget of billions. The DEA has been "fighting" this war for decades, but victory is nowhere in sight; in fact, it appears the drugs are winning.

The United States is the largest consumer of cocaine in the world, and the U.S. government concentrates much of its drug warfare resources on the cocaine trafficking from South America. "Plan Columbia" was a well-publicized operation, a multi-country strategy to shut down the cocaine trade. Over two billion dollars of military and police hardware was given to Columbia and many hundreds of millions more in military and technical equipment to other countries along the cocaine smuggling routes, including Costa Rica, Honduras, and Mexico.

Despite these efforts, the DEA manages to confiscate only a tiny percentage of the drugs smuggled. In fact, the cocaine market in the United States became saturated around 2006, and consumption has since declined slightly. In view of this, the question becomes, what happened to the "drug war" and where is it fought? Even more poignant, what's the point?

In the drug war, as in all wars, there is violence, corruption, and collateral damage. The violence and collateral damage occur most often on city streets; the corruption inside city hall and bank buildings. The vast profit margins of the cocaine trade—"washed" through the international banking system—allow for plenty of cash for bribes, "gifts," corrupt politicians, guns, and gunslingers.

Wars also result in collateral *benefits*. For example, in Vietnam and in recent wars with Iraq and Afghanistan, U.S. corporations and stockholders have benefitted enormously. There are also collateral benefits in the drug war, not only for the cartels, but also for the many thousands of DEA employees, corrupt officials, the world's banks, and ordinary citizens going about their business.

We observed the cocaine smuggling route adjacent to the southwest Pacific coast of Costa Rica—one of the most remote regions in Central America. We witnessed how the cocaine trade impacted the lives of local citizens living along the smuggling routes. This particular collateral benefit illustrates the surprising effects of unintentional consequences.

Cocaine traffickers are concentrated along the northwest coast of Columbia. From there, the cocaine begins its journey north to the United States. Although land travel is often used, it's risky because of all the border crossings. Water travel on the ocean, however, is wide open.

The smugglers carry more drugs than fuel, so they move the drugs in a series of short trips. Costa Rica is close enough to Columbia to serve as storage and transfer point. Even better, Costa Rica has no military, no high-tech radar centers, and almost no surveillance and interdiction capabilities. The U.S.

Coast Guard has a presence in these waters, and the Costa Ricans have three coast guard boats, but the ocean is vast.

The smuggling boats are fiberglass, long and wide, with high, strong bows to break through the waves and powered by three or four giant outboard motors. They usually carry from one to three tons of cocaine.

Occasionally, the coast guard will spot one of these boats and give chase. The standard response from the traffickers is to keep going full speed and throw the cocaine overboard. Sometimes these people are caught, but usually not. On rare occasions the packages of cocaine are recovered. (The traffickers have innovated; they've built "submerged vessels," which move just beneath the waves and are almost impossible to detect.)

The smugglers normally move the cocaine in packages of 20 kilos each, which is about 50 pounds and easy for one human to lift and carry. These packages are held together by black plastic wrapped with rope or twine, and are not waterproof. However, each individual kilo of cocaine typically is wrapped carefully in several layers of waxed paper and sheets of rubber and is waterproof.

Cocaine floats. The waves, currents, and tides disperse the packages quickly, and it's almost impossible for the Coast Guard to recover an entire load, especially if it's dumped at night. On several occasions we observed local boat captains recover one or more of these packages. Also, we saw locals recover kilos of cocaine that had washed up on the beaches.

These are locals and not heavy drug users and not interested in becoming dealers. However, in almost every case, they did not alert the authorities; instead, they elected to sell the cocaine. They usually sold the kilos to Costa Rican dealers in San Jose ($3,000 a kilo was the standard price). Given the small size of the country and a small, tight-knit population, it's not surprising the locals have little trouble making these sorts of clandestine connections.

The cocaine smuggling continues and people still find kilos occasionally. They tend to use the proceeds of these drug sales to invest in their businesses or improve their homes. Certainly they know that dealing in cocaine is illegal, but they insist they're not really dealing, they're not traffickers; they're simply taking advantage of an opportunity. We heard one boat pilot put it this way: "It's like hitting the lottery!" Twenty kilos of pure cocaine will bring around 60,000 dollars, a huge sum of money in these rural areas.

Again, unintended consequences also have consequences; although the locals typically see only the bright side of finding the cocaine—hitting the lottery—they rarely think about the effects these drugs may have on their fellow citizens or the stability of their country. The drugs are absorbed eventually into the population and cause unknown damage, misery, and death. Moreover, these consequences emphasize the global scale of the drug trade; cocaine is grown in Bolivia and Peru, processed in Columbia, smuggled through Central America, and eventually brought into the United States and Europe. Millions of people living along the cocaine smuggling routes are greatly impacted by the trafficking, even though they may have nothing to do with it.

According to the U.S. National Survey on Drug Use and Health (NSDUH), more than 22 million U.S. citizens aged 12 and older have used illegal drugs (2016). Marijuana was the most commonly consumed drug, followed by cocaine, hallucinogens, and methamphetamines.

Also, it is curious to note a substantial increase in people that used legal drugs illegally; that is, they obtained prescription drugs illegally, or they abused the drug that had been prescribed to them or someone else. A drug prescribed by a doctor and bought at a pharmacy is a legal transaction. This same drug acquired in a fraudulent or illegal manner, or used improperly, becomes illegal. Because of the nature of the drug, especially opioid analgesics, the patient may easily become addicted and abuse the drug. In the United States, over seven million people currently abuse legal drugs. The National Institute on Drug Abuse reported that there are more deaths annually attributed to overdose from prescription drugs than from heroin and cocaine combined (NIDA, www.drugabuse.gov).

Alcohol-related deaths in the United States are approximately 80,000 people each year. Alcohol causes nearly 50 percent of all non-fatal injuries and 20 to 25 percent of workplace injuries, costing around $100 billion a year—much more than cocaine or marijuana.

Although alcohol, if it is abused, is the most damaging drug, it is the only drug sold freely in most states to so-called "adults" without prescription or limit. Why is alcohol "legal" and other drugs are not? This curious fact was confusing to us until we discovered a symbiotic relationship between law enforcement agencies and the "illegal drug trade"; the existence of one justifies the existence of the other. On one side, billions in resources are received and spent by U.S. law enforcement to combat illegal drugs, employing thousands of people; on the other side, *because* the drugs are illegal, billions in profits are reaped by the "cartels" that invest and "wash" their cash through the international banking system. And in between, millions of people suffer violence, corruption, and social disintegration.

We now think that the illegality of certain popular drugs might be a method of social control, not unlike the earlier laws against opium smoking, except in this case the social control is applied to the general population. The United States has the largest prison population in the world, and most of those prisoners are minorities, and most of their "crimes" are drug-related. To bolster this hypothesis, we note that U.S. prisons are fast becoming "privatized," and prisoners are now considered a new corporate opportunity.

Corrections Corporations of America (CCA), as one example, is the largest private prison company in the United States. Their website maintains that "If you build it in the right place, the prisoners will come" (www.cca.com). CCA designs, builds, manages, and operates correctional facilities and detention centers on behalf of the Federal Bureau of Prisons, Immigration and Customs Enforcement, the United States Marshals Service, nearly half of all states, and nearly a dozen counties across the United States of America. Their website announces that CCA's president and CEO were featured in Forbes magazine.

The privatization of incarceration expands what is now called the prison industrial complex. Within private "correctional" corporations prisoners become a trapped labor force, with even fewer rights than in government-run facilities, and receive wages often lower than sweatshop workers in technologically underdeveloped countries. Private prison corporations typically are able to avoid giving prisoners worker benefits or the right to negotiate the conditions of their work or products. In our estimation, it's one step up from slavery.

In spite of claims about "rehabilitation," it is our assessment that people are sent to prisons—public or private—primarily as a form of *punishment*. They are segregated from society, stripped of most of their human rights, and confined within walls, behind bars, for years or for a lifetime. However, there is very little "rehabilitating." The primary lesson that prisoners learn well is how to survive under often tortuous circumstances. Any question of reintegration generally is simply a matter of time served, rather than restoration of character or social acceptance.

This punitive element of prison is supposed to reduce "crime" by acting as a deterrent. Indeed, it is logical to assume that people do not desire to spend years confined in prison, and yet how to account for continuing "crime" and the increase in prisoners? Clearly, other, more subtle social forces are at work in defining "crime" and applying "justice."

With the introduction of corporate, for-profit prison systems, the genesis of the prison as a place to be penitent is being replaced by a reinvented version of the Poor Law that demanded confinement in poorhouses or workhouses with coerced labor. The expanding prison industrial complex focuses on profit and cannot respond to the highly disproportionate number of prisoners from poor and/or minority communities. In fact, the more prisoners, the better. And in a further twist of bitter irony, the majority of these prisoners are convicted of drug-related crimes, yet while in prison they are able to obtain almost any drug through nefarious means or simply by buying it. Here again we encounter a situation that appears absurd, yet it is commonplace.

The corner drugstore is practically an American institution and exists throughout the Western countries. In a culture dedicated to "the pursuit of happiness," feeling bad or depressed is regarded as deviant, or "unhealthy," and some drugs make most people feel better. However, the corner drugstore, like the illegal drug trade, has grown into a giant corporate enterprise. Recent combined annual profits of the top ten prescription drug companies were nearly 90 billion dollars, an increase of 62 percent in only 10 years.

Current television and cable programs reveal a marked increase in advertisements for prescription drugs developed for possible ailments, and some ailments most humans never heard of ("hidden artery chewers," for example). These drugs come with exotic names formed out of clever juxtapositions of consonants and vowels. Most notably, these advertisements are directed straight at the consumer, not physicians or health workers. Smooth-voiced announcers ask viewers if they have the following "symptoms"; if so, it's likely they suffer from a certain condition. "Roloflex" will make them feel "normal" again—happy, healthy people! Of course, they should consult with their doctor and tell him about "Roloflex." (Imagine a TV commercial for *Oxybud Marijuana*: "Only one hit and you're good for the entire morning!")

In some cases, drug companies create and sell the ailment or disorder, and then sell the drugs to treat it. This is the complaint of Dr. Keith Conners, a psychologist and professor at Duke University. Professor Conners helped the effort to recognize attention deficit hyperactivity disorder (ADHD) among children as a special neurological problem. In 1996 the Food and Drug Administration (FDA) approved several CES drugs (central nervous system) for treatment of ADHD. Conners cited findings from the Centers for Disease Control and Prevention (CDC) showing that over 15 percent of high school students—around three and a half million—have been diagnosed with ADHD and are taking medication/drug therapy. Twenty-five years ago only 600,000 young people were diagnosed with ADHD. According to the CDC, ADHD is now the second most frequent long-term diagnosis made in children, following closely behind asthma. (Centers for Disease Control and Prevention, National Health Interview Survey, 2012). Conners (2013) called these rapidly rising rates of diagnosis "a national disaster of dangerous proportions...the numbers make it (ADHD) look like an epidemic. Well, it's not. It's preposterous. This is a concoction to justify the giving out of medication at unprecedented and unjustifiable levels" (p. 1).

The most commonly used drugs to treat ADHD are amphetamine-based stimulants that work on the central nervous system (CNS), altering cerebral and physical reactions. The most popular of these drugs is Adderall, made and marketed by Shire Incorporated, headquartered in Ireland, but marketing and selling drugs all over the world. Adderall and other CNS drugs that Shire produces sell extremely well in the U.S. market.

Shire operates similar to Monsanto, fostering close associations with universities, medical scientists, professors, and politicians. A Senate investigation in 2008 found that most research performed by Dr. Joseph Biederman, prominent child psychiatrist at Harvard University, had been funded by drug companies, including Shire, plus these companies paid Dr. Biederman over a million and a half dollars in speaking fees and "consulting." These facts are on the public record.

Dr. Biederman happens to be a staunch supporter of amphetamine drug therapy for children, especially the drug Adderall, but he has denied that the payments and research grants influenced his opinion. Nevertheless, Dr. Biederman's studies on ADHD and recommendations of particular drugs have been used extensively in advertisements and pamphlets distributed by drug companies—"A HARVARD PROFESSOR SAYS..." Typically, these studies demonstrate that ADHD is still under-diagnosed, that amphetamine stimulants are safe and effective, and, if not treated, ADHD-inflicted children have a high risk for school failure, drug abuse, car accidents, and legal troubles. None of these claims have been independently corroborated.

Drug companies also speak to youngsters directly. Shire, with several ADHD medications for sale, including bestselling Adderall, paid for the production of 50 thousand "comic books" that depict superheroes explaining about attention deficit disorder and what to do about it. These booklets were distributed free to patients with children.

Dr. Biederman and industry spokespersons describe CNS drugs as benign, even though they can have significant side effects. Moreover, these drugs are regulated in the same class as morphine and oxycodone because of their potential for abuse and addiction.

According to the CDC and Shire's own website, here are the most commonly reported side effects of taking Adderall, which may occur differently in each individual: bladder pain, bloody or cloudy urine, burning or painful urination, fast, pounding, or irregular heartbeat or pulse, frequent urge to urinate, lower back or side pain, anxiety, dry mouth, lack or loss of strength, stomach pain, weight loss, insomnia, headache, dizziness, nervousness, irritability, restlessness, unpleasant taste, nausea, euphoria, feelings of suspicion and paranoia, addiction, and tolerance (constant need to raise the dose). Less common side effects of Adderall are the following: constipation; decreased interest in sexual intercourse; false or unusual sense of well-being; loss in sexual ability, desire, drive, or performance; uncontrolled repetitive movements of the tongue, lips, face, arms, or legs; phonetic tics; high blood pressure; hallucinations; Tourette's syndrome; and death. Adderall is strongly suspected as the key ingredient in the deaths of twelve children.

Profits on sales of drugs for ADHD treatment have risen sharply. Last year they were approximately 10 billion dollars, more than five times they were 10 years ago. This growth is stimulated by drug companies marketing directly to doctors and by television and media advertisements that describe ADHD in broad, general terms, like "carelessness" or "impatience." Plus, they often exaggerate the drug's benefits—for example, highlighting the decrease in "family tensions," while downplaying the side effects. With the children's market in ADHD booming, the industry is using the same marketing techniques to concentrate on the adult version of ADHD. Private companies, operating as "legal" drug enterprises, attempt to influence the medical profession to increase the diagnosis of a particular medical condition in the interest of selling more drugs and making more profits.

Contributing to the sharp increase in prescription drug manufacture and consumption are demographic changes in the population. The largest segment of the population, the baby boomers, are now entering their sixties and seventies, and the natural process of aging brings on aches, pains, and a general deterioration of the body. Prescription drugs are there to help with these myriad physical maladies. There is also an increase of drug use to alleviate depression, anxiety, and other psychological conditions. Money spent on prescription drugs is still much more than is spent on illegal drugs.

Over one half the U.S. population uses prescription drugs. Also, U.S. consumers pay significantly more for prescription drugs than do consumers in any other country, even though the drugs are exactly the same. Per capita drug spending in the United States is about 40 percent higher than in Canada, 75 percent greater than in Japan, and nearly triple the amount spent in Denmark. Why is this if the drugs are virtually the same? We can only conclude that the U.S. market is controlled by a desire to wring maximum profits out of medical necessities.

The patenting of medicines, like the patenting of seeds, grants a virtual monopoly over the "controlled substances" available to consumers. Consistently higher drug costs contribute to significant increases in health care costs.

The majority of visits to doctors and outpatient clinics are to pick up another prescription or another order of drugs. The most often prescribed drugs are analgesics, which are pain killers generally, that often contain potent narcotic ingredients. There is no doubt that some prescription drugs have a significant positive impact on peoples' health, at least in the short term. Although drug costs are high, the consumption of some drugs may prevent much higher costs, such as hospitalization and surgery.

The U.S. culture is saturated with messages to consume and "be happy," and feelings of depression or "sadness" can induce a sense of guilt or shame, and trigger alarm and reaction. The purchase and consumption of mood-altering prescription drugs is attractive, if not exactly necessary. Obviously, those drugs that produce noticeable "highs" are typically the most in demand. These prescription "high" drugs are not organic, they're artificial. They target the psycho-mechanistic connections inside human brains and can dull or damage the body. Taken improperly, or sometimes properly, they can lead to seizures, heart attacks, respiratory collapse, and/or strokes.

The CDC report noted that doctors in private practices provided over *two and a half billion* drug prescriptions, more than five times as many as hospitals and clinics, and most of the drugs are pain killers or anti-depressants. From our perspective, there appears to be little difference between doctors and other drug dealers; they all sell "mood-altering" drugs for money, except doctor's deal openly and "legally." According to a study by Organization for Economic Co-operation and Development, prescriptions for anti-depressants have more than trebled since 1998 in the world's richest countries. (We hope to determine why so many humans in "rich countries" are diagnosed as "depressed.")

The profession of "medical doctor" has grown considerably in status and prestige since the last century, when earlier "healers" often sold "medicines" in liquid form with opium as the active ingredient. (We discovered a curious historical fact; the famous Rockefeller fortune in the United States was first begun by William Avery Rockefeller, a seller of such "herbal remedies.")

In the present, most humans regard doctors with confidence and respect; doctors heal people, or at least try. There is a deep-seated, traditional set of assumptions and attitudes attached to the identities of "doctor" and "patient." When people visit the clinic and enter the doctor's office, there are only two identities present and each identity is bound by the rules of the situation. The doctor examines, the patient complies; the doctor considers the possibilities, the patient waits hopefully or frightfully; the doctor makes a diagnosis and offers a remedy, the patient listens carefully, confident of the doctor's pronouncements and eager to begin therapy.

Increasingly, the therapy is drugs. The doctor may give the patient a few free samples he has received from a drug company representative, along with a bright, up-beat brochure explaining about the drug, its proper consumption, and any side-effects. And because the drugs are manufactured by a name-brand company and come from the doctor, most patients have confidence in them. This belief is also a common misconception among people who take prescription drugs for nonmedical purposes; because the drugs are legal they must be safe.

The face of the doctor is the face humans tend to trust, but the corporate enterprises behind the doctors remain unknown and out of sight. The doctor may care about people and may believe in the drug, but the corporation is dedicated to selling drugs for maximum profit. Private enterprise wants to sell as many prescription drugs as possible, and pushing them through doctors is an obvious strategy.

In this sense, prescription drugs are treated no differently from any other commodity, including the support of expensive promotional campaigns in the media. According to the Center for Public Integrity, drug companies spend around *20 times* more on marketing than on research and development (2016). Moreover, the drug industry has friends in high places. According to the same Center, from 1998 to 2007 drug companies spent around $850 million in lobbying the government—more than any other industry. In the U.S. presidential election of 2012, the drug companies donated millions as corporate PACs (political action committees), often to both candidates.

Drug salespersons visit doctors quite often to explain the latest drugs and their benefits, drop off a few free samples or "gifts," and even perform "favors." Sometimes, these visits are a help to doctors who are often quite busy and unable to keep up with the quickly expanding world of prescription drugs. However, there is also a definite marketing scheme involved in these relationships—a constant reminder and encouragement to prescribe certain drugs.

In conclusion, it is obvious that many humans like to get high, to take a break from their reality or for some other reason. Our reports note that he consumption of most drugs is usually a personal activity with little or no consequence to social stability, until the drug is abused, especially alcohol. However, defining drugs as "legal" or "illegal" pushes drug consumption into the realm of *political power*, where drug users and sellers can be controlled and manipulated. (Chiarello, 2015).

As a final note, we recognize another question we hope to investigate more fully; does privatized medical care and the exorbitant profits lead to more sick, unhealthy people—just as more prisons lead to more prisoners?

CHAPTER 4: WAR

A famous adage among the humans claims that war is politics by other means, and politics is supposed to be the process of governing. In our observations, however, we see that war is not governance. It is an extreme effort to control or eliminate other people, including their homes and resources. This is a curious characteristic of the human species. They are the only life-form on Earth that commits systematic genocide, not only against humans, but also against all other life-forms and the Earth itself.

They have a tendency to create "in" groups and "out" groups. The "in" group defines members of the "out" group as inferior beings, even genetically different—a separate, subspecies. In this way, killing the "out" group and stealing their resources is considered "rational" and morally acceptable. Human social scientists even have a name for this process; they call it "pseudo speciation"—that is, an *imagined* species.

How did humans on Earth adopt this behavior?

We understand that human history is supposed to be an accumulation of every individual's experience, and yet we find very little in the historical record about ordinary people living ordinary lives during years of peace. Instead, the written account of human history jerks and stops during peak times of frantic activity or crises—war, famine, disease, disaster—and it's usually the survivors, or victors, who control the perspective and write the bulk of history.

Human school books are punctuated by wars; the rise and fall of the Roman Empire, the Persian Empire, the Egyptian

Empire, the Hundred Years War, the War of the Roses, the wars of the Huguenots, the wars of the Crusades, England against France, England against Spain, France against Spain, Spain against the Inca and Maya, the European settlers against American Indians, the Spanish/American war, the U.S. Civil War, the numerous U.S. wars with the Philippines, Mexico, Haiti, Guatemala, Panama, El Salvador, Honduras, Chile; and there is the war between Japan and China, World War I and II, the Cold War, Korean War, Six Day War, Vietnam War, Nicaragua/Contra War, Iraq and Iran war, Russia/Georgia war, Afghanistan, Iraq, and Syria. This is only a small sampling.

In all these wars, most belligerents fought for one of two reasons—to conquer and dominate, or to defend against domination.

Such political conflicts occur constantly in human daily life as social groups and individuals try to manage their lives within the cacophony of demands made by the lives and desires of millions of others. Sometimes "social warfare" breaks out and people resort to violence. However, we notice that the economic and political leadership usually remain above the general conflict—and even control it, in some cases, by promoting particular agendas and ignoring others, or even creating tension and distraction by invoking racial/gender suspicions and animosities.

This process seems to be similar globally. There are many different nations on Earth, all competing for room to live and grow, the same as most citizens in those nations. Since Earth is a small world with finite resources and a human population of over seven billion, the control and extraction of resources has become desperate—to the point of violence and threats of violence and constant warfare.

Casting our observations around the world, we see wars occurring on every continent. The "motives" are often lost in the whirl of political spin, but the impacts are readily apparent;

dead and wounded bodies, burned villages and homes, buildings blown apart by rockets, artillery, and "smart bombs," precious lives and resources destroyed and squandered.

War is the most consumptive activity on earth. The world's biggest consumer of fuel is the U.S. military, followed by the military forces of other technologically developed nations. Also, the development of high-tech weapons systems demands constant extraction of special minerals and compounds, continuously destroying eco-systems, habitats, and indigenous populations. And, of course, there is the consumption of human lives, dreams, and futures.

Human history reveals how kings, tyrants, and governments purchased weapons of war and the soldiers to carry them. We discovered stories of kings rising or falling, dictators toppled and hung, and governments triumphant or defeated, but we saw very little about the *business* of weaponry. Someone had to make the armored suits and swords, the machine guns, the napalm bombs, the atomic bombs—and weapons don't come cheap.

The Manhattan Project during World War II cost the U.S. government over two billion dollars (30 billion in today's dollars), and when they finally had a workable bomb, someone was going to use it. A generation later the U.S. spent over 200 billion dollars conducting 15 years of warfare in Vietnam. At the time, this was the most expensive war in U.S. history, and yet it seems like a bargain compared to the several *trillion* dollars already spent in the invasions and occupations of Iraq and Afghanistan, and the ongoing warfare in Syria, Yemen, Iraq, Somalia, Ukraine, and Libya. (We see one more question to investigate; the *privatization* of the U.S. military.)

The Russians have been making war in Chechnya for 200 years. Their latest war in Chechnya has cost over 16 billion dollars, and now they are stationing troops on the Crimean Peninsula and threatening invasion of Ukraine. But their

GDP is ten times less than that of the United States. Chinese "defense" spending has increased substantially in response to the gravity of several territorial disputes with Japan and the Philippines. Also, Chinese armies continue to occupy Tibet and Mongolia. In 2012 their military spending was second only to that of the United States; over 100 billion dollars. The 30-year gas agreement between China and Russia creates an economic boost for them at a time when the United States and the European Union imposed sanctions against Russia and Europe threatening to cut its gas imports to punish the Kremlin over the continuing crisis in Ukraine.

However, our research suggests that we need a deeper, historical perspective. When the First World War ended and the troubles in Europe seemed over for the moment, the U.S. military and most military forces in the developed countries lay dormant for two decades (except Germany). Also, the economic depression in the United States continued to demand the attention of citizens and governments. Apart from Germany's feverish rearming, only a few private arms and ammunition factories continued to operate.

The onset of the Second World War and its outcome changed almost everything, including science, economics, politics, and geography. Science became the backbone of the military/industrial alliance; mass marketing and mass consumption transformed economies; political policy, particularly foreign policy, followed "the national interest"; new countries were created with borders that bore little resemblance to social realities on the ground. This outcome was fairly general among the "the victors" of the war—the United States, Western Europe, and Russia.

Unlike the exhausted peace following the earlier world war, the Second World War did not stop; it simply transformed into a new war—the cold war, with former allies now antagonists. Moreover, the transformation of the colonial system led to the birth of new nations, yet these nations were merely lines drawn on a map. Ethnic and kinship traditions were wholly ignored, almost ensuring constant conflict and instability. (Part of this problem may have been a deliberate strategy by Britain and the United States—the "mapmakers.")

Although the "hot" war was over, armies, navies, and air forces were still maintained at high alert and ready to attack, even with nuclear payloads. For decades, the "defense posture" between the United States and the Soviet Union had been based on the MAD doctrine—mutual assured destruction.

Yet, we note that humans no longer pay much attention to nuclear weapons and their destructive power. During the height of the Cold War, in the 1950s and '60s, U.S. school children regularly practiced "nuclear alerts." When the air raid sirens screamed, children jumped from their desks, crouched on the floor, and held papers and books over their heads. "Don't look out the windows," shouted the teacher. "The fireball may blind you!" There were also many public places—buildings, basements, tunnels, subways—that were clearly labeled as "Fallout Shelters," and citizens were encouraged to know where these shelters were located and the nearest evacuation routes out of the city.

However, today there is scant notice among the public toward nuclear weapons, and even less is known of their destructive power. We no longer see places designated as "Fallout Shelters." In fact, we found few references in the mainstream media related to nuclear explosions. The most credible report we discovered was in the 1962 issue of the *New England Journal of Medicine* entitled "The Medical Consequences of Thermonuclear War." A group of doctors and defense specialists had estimated the probable damage of a 20-megaton hydrogen bomb explosion over a heavily populated area. First, they examined the essential elements of the explosion—the blast effects, heat wave and levels of radiation—and then applied this information to a hypothetical nuclear attack on the city of Boston.

In one of the summaries we read this: "A 20-megaton ground burst on downtown Boston would seriously damage reinforced concrete buildings to a distance of ten miles. Within a circle of a radius of 16 to 21 miles, second degree burns would be produced, and clothing, houses, foliage, gasoline, and so forth would ignite, producing a fire storm. Human survival in this area would be practically impossible, and an estimated two million five hundred thousand deaths would occur in metropolitan Boston from blast and heat alone."

This was written in 1962, over 50 years ago! By now Boston has a more concentrated population—as do most large U.S. cities—and nuclear weapons have been "improved." The results today could only be much worse. While the United States appears to have the most nuclear weapons, Russia has many 20-megaton nuclear warheads targeted on the United States and possibly China. China also has a nuclear arsenal, slightly smaller than those of Russia and the United States, but in the realm of atomic destructive power "smaller" doesn't mean much. If all nuclear weapons were detonated at once, most of Earth's land mass would be destroyed and rendered uninhabitable for hundreds of years, entraining the extinction of humankind.

To live day-to-day with such a possibility may have psychological and emotional consequences for the humans. Perhaps, for this reason, nuclear weapons are kept hidden and hardly mentioned. It is as if their existence is too awful to contemplate; denial becomes more salient.

Humans described the cold war as entirely political; it was "democracy" versus "communism," and it played out on a global scale. But this cold war was not always cold. The ostensible motive for U.S. military involvement in Korea and Vietnam was "containment of communism," and these wars were definitely hot. During the Vietnam War the United States dropped more explosive tonnage—including chemical weapons—on Southeast Asia than was used by all sides during both world wars. The Soviet Union and China supplied North Vietnamese forces.

This was known as a "proxy war"—two dominant political ideals fighting their battles on the fields of a third country. Because of the certain death inherent in Mutual Assured Destruction, the two principle nuclear superpowers could not fight each other directly. For decades, until the Soviet Union dissolved, most of the world played host to one force or the other. Sometimes, these cold war conflicts appeared as public propaganda or disinformation campaigns; most often, however, they occurred inside the hidden world of clandestine operations, as each side tried its best to influence and coerce other governments and each other.

Occasionally, these secret machinations flared into public view when governments were suddenly toppled. In the early 1950s, during the height of the cold war, the United States engineered a coup d'état against two governments: Iran and Guatemala. We will report some of the details of these events because they reveal how lofty political ideals are sometimes used as smokescreens to obscure more mundane, practical motives, such as corporate profits, or access to vital resources. Moreover, Earth still lives with the consequences of these coups, especially in the case of Iran.

Britain had occupied Iran during World War Two, partly to protect the Allied supply route to the Soviet Union, but mainly to prevent Nazi Germany from obtaining the oil. After the war, Britain retained control of the oil through the Anglo-Iranian Oil Company. In 1951 the Iranian parliament voted to nationalize the oil industry. Mohammad Mosaddeq, an outspoken opponent of the British colonial posture, was elected Prime Minister and promised to carry through with nationalization.

The British appealed to the U.S. government for help. Clearly, Mosaddeq's intention to nationalize a private company revealed "communist tendencies." Indeed, the communist party in Iran gained some support through their opposition to the British, but Mosaddeq was not a communist; he described himself as a nationalist, as did others.

However, in the social atmosphere of the times, anything or anyone ostensibly connected to communism had to be confronted at once, according to U.S. political and military doctrine. Also, Britain was still rebuilding, and the United States was in the midst of rapid economic expansion, both efforts fueled in part by easy, cheap access to Iran's oil.

Allen Dulles, Director of the CIA, came up with a plan to get rid of Mosaddeq, which involved propaganda campaigns, paid demonstrations, recruitment of "disgruntled" army officers, and hiring sympathetic locals to stir up trouble. We discovered a curious footnote to this incident, which illustrates the importance of social class connections: CIA officials enlisted the help of Gen. H. Norman Schwarzkopf, the father of a future Persian Gulf War commander. Also involved was the CIA's chief of the Near East, Kermit Roosevelt, grandson of Theodore Roosevelt. The Secretary of State at this time was John Foster Dulles, Allen's brother.

The CIA plan went into effect. After a short, sharp period of unrest and disorder stirred up by CIA operatives, a reluctant Mohammad Reza Shah Pahlavi was installed as Shah (Palavi harbored a healthy distrust of the British, who had ousted his father in an earlier coup). Mohammad Mosaddeq, the popularly elected Prime Minister, was arrested, tried, and spent three years in prison. Gen. Fazlollah Zahedi, handpicked by the CIA and a Shah loyalist, was installed as the new Prime Minister. American and British oil corporations renewed their

Iranian operations under very favorable terms granted by the new Shah.

For 26 years, the extravagant Shah and his dreaded secret police, SAVAK, ruled ruthlessly over all aspects of Iranian life, with the support of the U.S. and British governments. Assassination, rape, torture, and imprisonment were used by SAVAK operatives to keep the Shah in power. (General Schwarzkopf organized the first security force, which evolved into SAVAK; later, the Israeli MOSSAD trained SAVAK personnel.)

Finally, in 1979 the Iranians rose up and kicked out the Shah and arrested members of the hated SAVAK. The revolutionary leader Ayatollah Khomeini returned triumphantly to Tehran from exile in France. Shortly after this, an angry Iranian population stormed the compound of the U.S. Embassy and took embassy personnel hostage. After a generation of living under the brutal suffocation of a Shah installed and supported with U.S. and British help, it is understandable why many Iranians might harbor serious resentments.

In the versions of this story that we've seen, oil was the primary concern of the U.S. and Europe. The struggle against communism provided the perfect cover and a public motive.

We encountered a similar story in 1951, also involving the U.S. CIA. The newly elected Guatemalan President Jacobo Arbenz intended to follow through with a broad land-reform program begun in the previous administration. At the heart of the program was the turn-over of unused land to landless farmers. At this time, 70 percent of all land was owned by only 2 percent of the population. United Fruit Company was the biggest landowner in Guatemala, owning over 42 percent of all arable land, most of which lay uncultivated. Arbenz offered to buy this uncultivated land from United Fruit Company for $600,000, an amount based on United Fruit's own tax assessments. However, United Fruit had severely underpriced the land to avoid taxes in the United States and Guatemala.

The company refused this offer and sought help from the U.S. government.

The Dulles brothers—John, Secretary of State, and Allen, Director of the CIA—held substantial shares in United Fruit. They were also staunch anti-communists, as were many U.S. citizens at this time. They regarded the act of giving away privately owned land to landless people as either bad business or "communism."

At first, Arbenz's land reform program was a success; in 18 months the government distributed 1,500,000 acres of unused land to about 100,000 families. President Arbenz also gave up 1,700 acres of his own land.

Meanwhile, the Dulles brothers reported to President Eisenhower that their agents had discovered communists inside the Arbenz administration, and they suspected Arbenz was under the direct control of Moscow. Again, as with Iran, there was a communist party in Guatemala, legally registered, but they held only four seats in the 58 member senate. Arbenz was not a communist; he was a member of the Revolutionary Action Party and admired the revolution that created the United States. U.S. leaders maintained, nonetheless, there were communists present in the Guatemalan government, and if they were allowed to gain a foothold, the whole region was in danger, including the United States.

The CIA set into motion its plan to get rid of Arbenz—a massive misinformation campaign, recruitment of ambitious military commanders and paid political agitators and demonstrators. Eventually, Arbenz was forced to resign and fled into exile in Mexico. A military junta was installed, and United Fruit was safe, at least for the next few decades (at that time, Guatemalan bananas made up a fourth of the company's production).

According to the CIA's own written history, independent analysts sifted through over one hundred and fifty thousand government documents, searching for proof that Arbenz was directed by the Soviet Union. The only solid reference they found was a receipt for $22.95 to the Guatemalan communist party from a book shop in Moscow.

This sort of gigantic miscalculation—or misrepresentation—was most used to justify the U.S. invasion of Iraq. Western intelligence agencies insisted Iraq was building weapons of mass destruction and "regime change" was necessary. After the invasion, no such weapons were found. We find it interesting that the CIA can be so effective in one place and so inefficient in other places. We've decided that the CIA's apparent enlightenment or ignorance might be a deliberate position.

Once the Arbenz administration had been overturned, a military dictatorship took over, and for the next 30 years Guatemala was ruled by a succession of dictatorships, which tended to make war on their own citizens—by most estimates, killing over one hundred thousand, many of them Mayan Indians.

Guatemala has not recovered to this day. The chance at democracy and true land reform was denied to the Guatemalan people because of the sacred status of private property and corporate operations. The public motive, however, was the "war against communism."

Today in Guatemala the huge gap between rich and poor still exists. Although it is one of the poorest countries in Latin America, it hosts a small, rich elite that control most land and industry.

It is worth reflecting for a moment on the consequences of these cold war actions by the U.S. military-industrial complex. An alliance between private interest and political power spearheaded operations to depose popularly elected foreign governments and impose brutal dictatorships. The entire populations of two countries were oppressed for decades, with the help and encouragement of the U.S. government. And now the consequences are still causing problems. Guatemala remains in the tight grip of the landed aristocracy, and Iran harbors anger and distrust toward the United States, Britain, and Israel.

We want to report one other U.S. involvement in Latin America, which is slightly different and illustrates the casual regard of U.S. leaders toward smaller sovereign states—in this case, Panama. The nation of Panama used to be the northern province of Columbia, but the United States engineered the creation of the new country to protect the strategic integrity of the Panama Canal. Ever since, the United States has maintained political dominance and a military presence in Panama.

Manuel Noriega was a career officer in the Defense Forces of Panama and attended the School of the Americas at Fort Benning in the U.S. state of Georgia. During the 1960s and '70s, Noriega was an officer in the Panamanian army and a paid informant of the CIA. He also worked closely with the U.S. Drug Enforcement Administration in the "war on drugs."

Eventually, Noriega became President of Panama. The President of the United States, George W. Bush, had been Director of the CIA and Vice President; therefore, he knew Manuel Noriega had been a CIA operative, and he knew Noriega had become involved with drug traffickers, mainly in laundering their illicit profits. However, because Noriega was a staunch supporter of the U.S. government, a "valuable" CIA informer and DEA undercover agent, his illicit activities were ignored. However, when these activities became public, the Bush Administration immediately stepped back from Noriega and pressured him to resign.

After a few months of public threats and insults, Noriega appealed for military assistance from the Soviet Union, Cuba, and Nicaragua. This was a fatal mistake. For nearly 100 years, Panama had supported the United States—either voluntarily or not—but now Manuel Noriega was reaching out to so-called "communist governments." It was time for "regime change."

The removal of Noriega was different from other "regime changes" executed by the United States. This time it was not a clandestine attack by the CIA; rather, U.S. military forces invaded Panama, overran the country, subdued the army, and kidnapped President Noriega. Although the method of "regime change" was different, the public justification was very similar; according to President Bush, the removal of Noriega was necessary "to protect American lives and the national interest."

We highlight these stories because they reveal a pattern for other cold war foreign involvements by the CIA and the U.S. military. The attempted coup against President Castro, the infamous "Bay of Pigs" incident, was a failure, but the coup against President Diem of South Vietnam was successful. A coup in Chile against Salvador Allende, another popularly elected president, also succeeded, orchestrated by Henry Kissinger, President Nixon's Secretary of State. In this particular "regime change," president Allende was replaced by Gen. Augusto Pinochet, another military dictator, who not only repressed his own citizens, but also participated in a region-wide "black war" against political dissidents. (The sins of Augusto Pinochet fall heavily on the head of Henry Kissinger.)

Incidentally, our investigations have uncovered millions of U.S. diplomatic and intelligence documents from 1973 to 1976 known as the "Kissinger cables." These documents tell the story of Kissinger's involvement in a series of alleged war crimes in Indochina, Bangladesh, Chile, Cyprus, and East Timor. He is accused of direct interference in these governments, in which military operations resulted in thousands of casualties. Moreover, legal representatives in Chile, Argentina, Spain, and France continue to call for Kissinger to testify about his involvement in the coup in Chile. A Chilean judge has asked Kissinger to answer written questions about this event and his relationship with General Pinochet.

Ironically, Kissinger was awarded the Noble Peace Prize, one of Earth's most prestigious prizes. Now, however, many countries are calling for Kissinger to replace his Peace Prize with the War Prize.

The U.S. public motive for military involvement in Vietnam was "containment of communism." Actually, our research has discovered that Ho Chi Minh wrote letters to U.S. Presidents Eisenhower and Kennedy asking for their help in the Vietnamese struggle against French colonial forces. Ho equated Vietnam's fight for independence against France with the U.S. revolutionary war against the British Empire. Ho was not a communist; he was a nationalist, a revolutionary fighting against French colonial rule.

Eisenhower and Kennedy ignored Ho's pleas, probably to appease their French allies. Eventually, Ho was forced to seek help from the Soviet Union and China. After the defeat of the French forces, the U.S. military-industrial complex stepped into the fight. The public motives were stated clearly; if communism wasn't stopped decisively in Vietnam, a "domino effect" would occur, and the whole of Southeast Asia could be "lost"—that is, converted to communism.

It's been difficult for us to ascertain the other motives for U.S. involvement in Vietnam, other than to pay close attention to two obvious outcomes of the war: One, several Southeast Asian nations had been bombed into wreckage and were no longer attractive as an ally to anyone. Two, most of the $200 billion the U.S. government spent in conducting the war went straight into the coffers of U.S. corporations. (Incidentally, the cost of the war created the first U.S. balance-of-payments deficit of the twentieth century.)

Although our observations have concentrated on the most powerful country on Earth, other powerful countries also engage in the interference and manipulation of foreign governments. For example, the Soviet Union had invaded

Czechoslovakia, Hungary, Georgia, Afghanistan, and Crimea. By far the most costly engagement for the Soviets was the Afghan war. The Soviet Union had a long history of involvement in Afghanistan, dreaming of friendly access to India, warm ocean ports, and Central Asian markets (sometimes called the "Middle East"). For years a Soviet-backed Afghan government ruled through repression and corruption, but in 1979 an uprising began that threatened to overturn the regime. Moscow claimed that the Afghan Prime Minister Hazifullah Amin, their hand-picked man, had invited the Soviet army into Afghanistan to help crush a rebellion led by "Islamic militants." In statements to the Soviet public, the government explained that the army had to enter Afghanistan to "protect and liberate" the communists.

Meanwhile, the United States took this opportunity to attack their cold-war enemy indirectly by arming and training the Afghan rebels. This may be regarded as another "proxy war," where two world powers fight their battles inside a third country. It was during this time that the CIA made an arrangement with Osama bin Laden, one of the chief leaders of the rebellion and destined to become the "mastermind" of the "terrorist attacks" of September 2001 in the United States.

The Soviets, like the Americans in Vietnam, were surprised at the ferocity of rebel resistance, and got sucked into a "never-ending war," especially while the United States and other countries supplied the rebels with sophisticated weapons. For eight years they fought a losing battle and finally withdrew in 1989. According to official claims, over 15 thousand Soviet soldiers were killed and nearly one hundred thousand wounded. The monetary costs of the war are not known, but reckoned to be considerable. In any case, most political analysts argue that the folly and expense of this war influenced the subsequent break-up of the Soviet Union. And periodically, Russia sends occupation troops to the Crimea Peninsula, and the reason usually is the same—to "protect Russians" from Ukrainian mobs.

These stories illustrate how Earth's governments justify foreign involvements with political ideals, often expressed in patriotic language. However, beneath the surface we find more profane reasons for foreign intervention—controlling key geopolitical positions, assuring access to markets and resources, and making the world safe for corporations.

When the Soviet Union broke up, other countries also gained independence—the reunification of Germany and nation states in Eastern Europe. These events were generally recognized as the collapse of communism, or at least it no longer carried credibility and was no longer considered a threat to the "free world."

However, just as the "communists" stepped off the world stage, the "terrorists" arrived. According to our research, terrorists have been around a long time, but usually along the fringes of political conflict. Also, the definition of "terrorist" keeps changing. For example, Nelson Mandela, a famous and popular political dissident, was for many years considered a "terrorist." Now he's a hero. Even Gandhi, a revolutionary famous for his non-violent approach, was described once by British leaders as a "terrorist." J. Edgar Hoover, Director of the FBI, kept close surveillance of Martin Luther King, whom Hoover regarded as an agitator, traitor, and communist. The leaders of the American Revolution, including George Washington, were regarded by the British as traitors and rebels and would have been "terrorists" if the word was in vogue.

However, with the events of September 11, 2001, the identity of "terrorist" stepped out of the shadows and into the world's spotlight. U.S. President George Bush described the perpetrators as "terrorists" and "evildoers." In this regard, the Bush Administration did not admit publicly that this "terrorist act" was *political*. By disregarding the political nature of the act, the U.S. leadership denied everyone, including the American people, a bit of enlightenment and reality: The history of the U.S. military-industrial complex in Central Asia is a policy of heavy-handed domination, especially in regards to Palestinians.

The United States invaded Afghanistan to eliminate the "terrorists." The United States invaded Iraq because Saddam had "weapons of mass destruction" and he might give them to "terrorists." (This accusation from a country armed with six thousand nuclear warheads.) Russia found "terrorists" in Chechnya and Georgia. China identified "terrorists" among the monks in Tibet. Columbia re-defined the Revolutionary Armed Forces of Columbia (FARC) as "terrorists" (they used to be "communists"). In Mexico we find a hybrid—a "narco-terrorist."

A whole series of repressive measures have occurred during the "war on terrorism." For example, airports around the world have been forced to change and strengthen security. All intelligence agencies have stepped up their surveillance of each other and everyone. The U.S. military often commits murder on the soil of several sovereign nations by shooting drone-launched Hellfire missiles at people. The government and the media call the targets "suspected terrorists." (We point out that "suspected terrorists" could also be "suspected civilians.")

Since the identity of "terrorist" is fluid and constantly changing, we hope to focus our investigation on the social conditions and political processes that maintain, create, and change the definitions of certain actions as terrorist. In this way we might better understand terrorism as a particular social event within a particular social context (Bergen, 2016).

For example, the U.S. invasion of Iraq offers a provocative demonstration of how political ideals and threats of "terrorism" can be used to justify warfare against a sovereign state. The Bush Administration argued that Saddam Hussein was building "weapons of mass destruction" and was likely to give them to "terrorists." The United States was obliged to force "regime change" in Iraq to protect American citizens. It was in the "national interest."

However, our research demonstrates that forceful removal of Hussein was advocated three and half years *before* the attacks on 9/11. A prominent think tank called The Project for a New American Century sent a letter to former President Clinton urging him to force Saddam Hussein from power because he was a bad guy and building weapons of mass destruction. The letter cautioned President Clinton not to pay too much attention to the United Nations because American policy cannot continue to be crippled by a misguided insistence on unanimity in the UN Security Council. Of the 18 people who signed this letter, 10 eventually became members of the Bush cabinet. The events of 9/11 offered the ideal opportunity for these people to carry forward the plan for "regime change" in Iraq. However, since Iraq had nothing to do with the attacks in New York and Washington, DC, a different, "plausible" motive for invasion had to be constructed.

Here again, we see how patriotic ideals and dire warnings are used in justifying the call for warfare. After the invasion, the Bush Administration searched high and low in Iraq, but found no weapons of mass destruction. (It's highly likely they knew they weren't there in the first place.) No matter; as President Bush proclaimed—"mission accomplished." But what was the mission? We know the public motives for the Iraqi invasion, but what were the other reasons? Again, by paying attention to the outcome of the invasion we find clues to other motives—for the first time in decades the United States has a military presence in Iraq, a working embassy/fortress, a strong, strategic position to confront Iran and control of the oil.

The U.S.-led wars in Iraq and Afghanistan, with their "shock and awe" tactics, the legal atrocity of prisoners indefinitely detained at Guantanamo by the world's "freest society," and the reemergence of lone-wolf terrorism have introduced Earth's people to a modern American morality play. This is a crossroads of politics and deviance where social and moral boundaries distinguish public virtue from dangerous deceit.

In regards to dangerous deceit, advances in technology have not only introduced vastly improved methods of communication—such as cell phones and the Internet—but also greatly enhanced methods of surveillance and intelligence gathering. Here again, the irony of science and technology is revealed, as it was with the splitting of the atom: The great convenience and wonder of instantaneous communication of information has been turned into a weapon against human dignity and privacy.

One of the biggest news stories in 2013 was the revelation that the U.S. National Security Agency (NSA) has been spying on millions of American citizens and foreign citizens and their governments, including close allies. This surveillance began shortly after the "terrorist attacks" on the United States in September 2001. At that time, President George Bush approved an expanded intelligence gathering program called initially the "President's Surveillance Program," which ostensibly was targeted at identifying and locating "terrorists."

For the first few years this program was kept secret, but in 2005 *The New York Times* reported that the NSA conducted surveillance activities within the United States. At that time, the Bush Administration admitted the existence of what it called the "Terrorist Surveillance Program" in which the NSA supposedly monitored communications of around one thousand people inside the United States with "suspected connections" to Al Qaeda—the organization allegedly responsible for the attacks of September 2001.

However, it wasn't until June 2013 that the full extent of NSA surveillance was revealed, principally by Edward Snowden, a former employee of the CIA and private contractor with the NSA (Gellman, 2016). According to documents released by Snowden, NSA domestic surveillance activities were much more widespread than government officials had admitted. Apparently, the NSA had convinced most major U.S. telecommunications companies to turn over millions of citizens' phone records, including their names, addresses, and other personal data. In addition, the NSA monitored the principle internet carriers—Google, Microsoft, Facebook, Yahoo, YouTube, AOL, and Skype—and collected hundreds of millions of email messages and contact lists from personal email accounts and instant messaging services.

These revelations caused an immediate storm of protest within the United States and among foreign governments, especially those targeted by NSA surveillance. Spying on U.S. citizens is prohibited by law and by constitutional amendment. Spying on foreign governments, including presidents and prime ministers, violated diplomatic protocol and treaty agreements, as well as damaged friendly relations. In its defense, the NSA claimed it had presidential approval and congressional oversight. Plus, it asserted that these surveillance activities had resulted in preventing "several terrorist attacks." However, these claims do not make such surveillance legal, and congressional oversight committees have denied knowing the full extent of NSA domestic spying activities.

Snowden apparently "appropriated" over a million secret documents from NSA archives, and these are being released little-by-little through various select newspapers and media organizations. Each new release evokes fresh allegations against the NSA and charges of abuse, not only from U.S. lawmakers and citizens, but also foreign governments. For example, revelations that the NSA monitored the phone conversations of German Chancellor Andrea Merkel and members of her cabinet resulted in a burst of outrage from Ms. Merkel and most German citizens.

Although Snowden has been hailed as a hero by some and praised for his courageous actions, he has also been called a "traitor." Snowden had been bound by oaths of secrecy, and he broke those oaths, which in this case is a formal crime. American authorities have charged him with espionage and theft of government property. We find this to be an interesting irony; Snowden is charged with espionage for revealing the extent of NSA espionage (Gellman, 2016).

The NSA also works closely with the CIA in its program of "targeted assassinations," most of which have occurred in Central Asian countries where American troops are not welcome. These assassinations are usually carried out by pilotless "drone" aircraft that are operated by remote control by U.S. military personnel known as the Joint Special Operations Command (JSOC). Most of these operators sit inside small, container-sized air conditioned units located thousands of miles from the "targets."

By locating and monitoring the Subscriber Identity Modules (SIM cards) inside cell phones, the NSA can access the personal information of the account holder, including phone number; address book, text messages, and other data. The NSA can locate the approximate position of a "target" anywhere in the world through the Global System for Mobile Communications (GSM) network. If the SIM card is thought to be carried by the "target" and his or her location is verified by satellite image, a Hellfire missile or other destructive device is launched at the "target."

However, such targeted assassinations have drawn indignation and protest from several governments and civil rights organizations, mainly because of the impossibility of positive identification of "targets" and the indiscriminate nature of the explosive device. Several incidents have been recorded in which "mistakes" occurred and "smart missiles" missed their target or hit the wrong target and killed or injured innocent civilians. These "targeted assassinations" by the NSA and CIA, plus the revelations of widespread surveillance of domestic and foreign citizens, have severely damaged the reputation and integrity of the United States government.

Among Snowden's most recent release of documents are the revelations that the British intelligence service and NSA personnel somehow recorded "webcam" images from millions of users of Yahoo. The NSA justified this monitoring by stating it was "searching for suspected terrorists," but according to the documents, most of these images contained photos and videos of a private nature among families and individuals, including some with sexual content.

Moreover, there are allegations that NSA personnel have also engaged in industrial espionage by monitoring the private communications of foreign corporations. Clearly, this form of espionage is intended to gain an economic advantage for U.S. industry and has nothing to do with "terrorist activities." In fact, it is alleged that NSA personnel have even used their espionage capability to spy on girlfriends, boyfriends, wives, and husbands.

In our efforts to investigate the NSA and confirm allegations of indiscriminate spying we encountered the same wall of secrecy that has stymied congressional and citizen inquiries. Therefore, we found it necessary to use our superior technology to spy on the NSA. We uncovered several curious components of this organization.

The NSA, as any bureaucratic entity, is a centralized power structure, with authority administered from top to bottom. However, the NSA is cloaked in a dark shroud of secrecy, and this secrecy seems concentrated toward the bottom. The public image of the NSA, like the upper level of an iceberg, pokes up into plain view, where the names and faces of top officials are known. But the vast secret workings of the organization are hidden below the surface. In this case, power flows from top to bottom, while secrets flow from bottom to top. In consequence, the secret, lower echelons of the NSA operate fairly independently from the power structure, allowing greater potential for abuse.

For example, we noticed how Private First Class Jones monitored the emails of his girlfriend, Ms. Pemberton, and discovered she was communicating secretly with Steven Phillips, including sexually explicit photos. As a result, PFC Jones terminated his relationship with Ms. Pemberton, but had great difficulty in explaining why. In a more serious incident, Corporal Smith located the SIM signal of a "high profile target" in Yemen, a man they had been tracking for three years. Corp. Smith reported the coordinates to his superior, Sergeant Schumacher. Sgt. Schumacher adjusted the satellite image and saw a group of armed men in close proximity to the signal. He verified the "target" to Corp. Smith and Corp. Smith fired a Hellfire missile toward the source of the SIM signal. However, the cell phone was in possession of the "target's" sister located two hundred meters away. The missile slammed into a wedding party, killing 23 people and injuring 50.

In response to allegations of widespread domestic surveillance, President Obama and other government officials have repeatedly denied that the NSA monitors the "contents" of phone conversations or emails. However, in most cases, these denials have had to be retracted by evidence revealed in the release of further documents by Snowden. Although there are laws governing restrictions on domestic spying, NSA secrecy is so extensive no one is really sure what exactly is going on. At this time there are several congressional investigations into NSA domestic surveillance, and a number of civilian organizations are filing lawsuits against the federal government for violation of privacy laws and civil rights.

It is our understanding that massive surveillance of civilian communications and behavior is incompatible with democratic and free societies. Such misuse of technology offers great potential for abuse by the political leadership, and such abuse has already been identified and verified by the disclosures of NSA internal documents.

In a deeper sense, these disclosures highlight a troubling component in the human character—if a powerful new technology is possible, then some humans will build it and use it, and not always peacefully or to social benefit. The development of nuclear weapons is one powerful example; the inappropriate use of communications technology is another.

We can relate to these issues. During our history we also faced such challenges with the development of new technologies. After several close-calls and near-disasters, we eventually solved this problem by introducing a much greater emphasis on collective learning, our symbiotic relationship with nature, and studying justice in our educational programs. Although scientific knowledge and technology will offer possibilities for abuse, *how* such technologies are used depends mainly on the moral character of a society.

If the humans survive their present difficulties and dangers, they too may solve this problem by educating their children to recognize the best moral choices. In this we have confidence and optimism since most humans have a fair understanding of moral priorities, unlike their governments and most corporate entities. Also important are "moral entrepreneurs"—such as Edward Snowden, Julian Assange (founder of WikiLeaks), Daniel Ellsberg, Mark Klein, William Binney, and Bradley Manning. The debate on whether they are patriots or traitors (political deviants or deviants) reveals much about the state of hegemony in the United States.

Finally, we should mention the close relationship between the U.S. military and private corporations. The dangers of this relationship were first recognized and described by President Dwight Eisenhower in his farewell address to America after two terms as president:

> In the councils of government, we must guard against the acquisition of unwarranted influence, whether sought or unsought, by the military-industrial complex. The potential for the disastrous rise of misplaced power exists and will persist. We must never let the weight of this combination endanger our liberties or democratic processes. We should take nothing for granted. Only an alert and knowledgeable citizenry can compel the proper meshing of the huge industrial and military machinery of defense with our peaceful methods and goals, so that security and liberty may prosper together... The prospect of domination of the nation's scholars by Federal employment, project allocation, and the power of money is ever present and is gravely to be regarded. (1961)(www.eisenhower.archives.gov/farewell)

President Eisenhower's warning did not succeed in "alerting the citizenry," mainly because the majority of citizens are kept ignorant about the activities of the military/industrial complex, especially within the secret boundaries of "national security." The research, development, and procurement of military equipment and weapons systems are rarely exposed to public view or even congressional scrutiny. The Pentagon's budget requests routinely contain secret allotments to private corporations. (The Pentagon budget [2016] was for half a trillion dollars, over fifty percent of total U.S. government spending.)

Most troubling in this process is the practice of "revolving door" employment—that is, retired military personnel and other top government employees stepping from government service directly into corporate positions, most often in the defense industry. One glaring example we found is the Carlyle Group, a giant private equity firm based in Washington, DC. Carlyle has learned the advantage of hiring former top government employees, including former presidents, secretaries of state, and top Pentagon and Defense Department officials. The Carlyle management invites potential investors to lunch or dinner with a former president or secretary of state, thus gaining the investors' confidence and often their money. Even more valuable, these former high profile government employees often retain direct contacts with current government officials, both military and civilian, and have little trouble helping their clients gain access to powerful decision makers.

Although this process of manipulation and access has been going on for decades, it has accelerated considerably since the attacks of September 11, 2001. The establishment of the new bureaucracy Homeland Security, with a budget of billions of dollars, has created new opportunities for abuse and advantages for private corporations, especially those engaged in telecommunications, electronics, and weapons research. Involved in this process is the continued privatization of the U.S. military, principally the Army. One reason why the invasions and occupations of Iraq and Afghanistan have been so expensive is the increased "outsourcing" of support facilities and supplies to private corporations.

Only three decades ago, the U.S. Army was a self-contained organization. Apart from combat personnel, there were also electricians, carpenters, clerks, cooks, drivers, bodyguards, police, stevedores, and mechanics. Now most of these support activities are performed by private contractors, which are paid much higher salaries than Army personnel. Recent

U.S. military adventures have greatly benefited private corporations and their shareholders, but it's impossible to know for sure to what extent these adventures may have been motivated in part by opportunities for profit and advantage.

Not only is war the most consumptive activity on Earth, but it is also practiced in the service of further consumption. Human warfare is conducted under a hegemonic banner of political and moral righteousness, but political power and economic consumption are the real motivators. War among the humans appears to be a means of taking what they want or need from other humans. The hegemonic character of the U.S. is plainly visible, for example, when President Obama declares publicly that President Assad of Syria "must resign immediately." In fact, the U.S. and other Western countries are involved in the current Syrian "civil war"—either directly or by supporting rival factions. Russia is also involved directly, since Syria is also a strategic asset for Moscow. Although all sides talk publicly about "justice" and "peace," the real, "practical," issue is the question of the future trajectory of an oil pipeline to Europe. At stake are billions of dollars and control of much of the area's oil reserves. So far, thousands have been killed, millions have been driven from their homes, and refugees fleeing the fighting choke the entrances to Europe.

With an ever-growing global population, and with demand for "consumer goods" increasing rapidly—in China, India, Brazil, and other countries—there is a corresponding rise in the global scramble to claim geographic areas known to contain essential resources. When we couple these resource tensions with traditional cultural fears and animosities, we predict Earth will experience a significant increase in warfare.

However, we want to point out two notable exceptions where relatively recent political activity has taken positive steps toward lasting peace. These exceptions are notable for different reasons: one because of the longevity of the political repression and conflict; the other for its non-violent ingenuity. They illustrate how moral boundaries separate political deviants who challenge the status quo for a higher moral good, versus deviants who primarily act for selfish reasons.

In the first case, Burma/Myanmar had endured six decades of political repression and social upheaval inflamed by global economic pressures, ethnic coercion, and armed conflicts. One of the world's longest conflicts results in untold sufferings for the Burmese people, which include loss of livelihood, massive internal displacements, external migration, and the exodus of refugees. However, a new sense of political spring has begun to bloom as the Burmese leadership opens up possibilities for the politics of multi-polarity, ethnic reconciliation, and democratic representation.

The other event is notable because of its simplicity and effectiveness. The Zapatista indigenous movement in Mexico evolved over time into a de facto "nation." After decades of resistance to the encroachment of Mexican federal authority and local and global corporate interests, these Indians resorted to a brief period of self-defense that was violent. However, this type of self-defense only aggravated the conflict and earned international sympathy for the Mexican government. Also, there were numerous attempts by local and global interest to define the Zapatistas as "terrorists."

In response, the Zapatistas renounced the use of violence and faded silently into their own territory. Over the years, with quiet, laborious work, they have built 32 autonomous, self-governing municipalities. Local representatives from Juntas de Buen Gobierno, or Councils of Good Government, preside over these independent Zapatista communities. The councils oversee community programs that distribute food, set up clinics and schools, and collect taxes. Resources are for those who live in the communities, not for the organizations or the corporations that come to exploit them.

Of course, these "councils" are not formally recognized by the Mexican government, which claims sovereignty over all Zapatista territory. However, the government also recognizes the advantages of allowing the councils to continue "governing"; if social stability is maintained and no army or police resources need be expended.

In terms of novel execution and extraordinary patience, the Zapatistas have formed the most important resistance movement of the last two decades. They are a visible counterbalance to the despoiling and rape of the planet and the subjugation of the poor by global economic relationships. They believe global corporations launched a war against the planet, and their quiet, non-violent determination has taught the world how to overcome these powerful political and corporate pressures. Zapatistas give global resistance movements a new language—drawn in part from the indigenous communal life—by offering an example and a new paradigm for political action and change.

Finally, one of the most troubling aspects of Earthly warfare is that constant technological innovation delivers more sophisticated, powerful weapons into the hands of all combatants, which increases the number of casualties, especially among civilians. Most of the Earth's militaries refer to civilian casualties as "collateral damage"; for example, when civilians are present at a particular place where a "smart missile" explodes on a nearby military target. "Smart missiles" are supposed to know where they're going, but their explosive power is ignorant and indiscriminate; they kill civilians and children as well as "terrorists." Saudi Arabia, making war in Yemen, is fond of U.S. supplied "cluster bombs," which spray deadly "bomblets" over several hundred meters, killing indiscriminately. The killing of many civilians, including children, in the "war on terror" motivates some of the survivors to strike back, often to become labeled as "terrorists."

Within this war context, we point out that there are approximately 20 thousand nuclear warheads on Earth—ranging from gigantic "doomsday" warheads of 50 megatons to small, "battlefield" nuclear warheads of a few kilotons. Most of these weapons are poised and ready for launch. We calculate that if only half these nuclear devices were to be detonated at once, most of Earth's landmass would be destroyed.

It is our estimation that the human race has reached a milestone in its evolutionary position on planet Earth. The combined effects of global warming, changing weather patterns, resource scarcity, and nuclear firepower have pushed humans into the territory of extinction. In fact, Earth's ecology is already experiencing a mass extinction event.

Planet Earth balances on a precarious pivot point in its existence. Its future lies between two extremes: social justice and abundance for all, or a slow, inexorable decent into planetary destruction. We calculate there is still time for humans to reduce consumption, repair the ecology, and save their world, but only if they begin a serious effort immediately.

CHAPTER 5: NEOLIBERALISM

The twin philosophies of constant consumption and market supremacy have had a critical impact on Earth's social systems and environment. Several decades ago, among top government and business leaders in Britain and the United States, a political idea called "neoliberalism" emerged and invaded all media and cultural outlets. Neoliberalism is the belief that market forces and private interests are the best determinants of the public good. By now, an entire generation has grown up with neoliberal ideals and often accepts them just as readily as they accept all other "realities" inside the Cultural Model.

However, as with other such "realities," neoliberalism is not an inherent principle of the social universe; it is merely a plan created and nourished by a particular "class" of people. Also, it has a history; there was a time when the ideas of neoliberalism held no sway and, in fact, would have been considered dangerous or crazy.

By 1945, the United States had been through a decade of depression, and the world had just fought a war, disrupting trade systems and international banking. New economic policies were needed on both the domestic and international levels. In the United States, the lessons and excesses of the 1920s and 1930s had bolstered the arguments of John Maynard Keynes, an influential U.S. economist. Keynes advocated more government regulation and intervention in the economy. By implementing certain policies, the government could lower unemployment, raise wages, and increase demand for "consumer goods." In this system, the State enforces a compromise between business and labor, which will ostensibly encourage economic growth and social stability.

The result was called "embedded liberalism," which was focused on setting a decent wage for working men and women and social welfare programs. These ideas were "embedded" in the ideal of "life, liberty, and the pursuit of happiness," which supposedly was at the heart of the American Dream. Labor unions were organized and encouraged, and were seen as counterweights to abusive business practices. Unemployment benefits and other social programs were developed to help those most in need. The implementation of these programs necessitated a graduated tax system, with a higher burden on the rich and corporations.

At the international level, policymakers applied the same sorts of Keynesian principles, hoping to smooth out balance of payment problems and encourage reconstruction and development in war-torn Europe. They created the Bretton Woods Institutions (which would later evolve into the World Bank, the International Monetary Fund, and the World Trade Organization.)

According to a press release by the Bretton Woods Conference (1944), "The world's nations should consult and agree on international monetary changes which affect each other. They should outlaw practices which are agreed to be harmful to world prosperity, and they should assist each other to overcome short-term exchange difficulties" (p. 193). The conference introduced fixed exchange rates with built-in flexibility for difficult times and encouraged "open markets" by lowering trade barriers. It was hoped these changes would foster international economic and social stability and prevent another world war.

For the next three decades, these policies led to unprecedented growth in consumption levels for millions of people, in both Europe and the United States. The share of wealth to the top 1 percent in the United States fell from 16 percent to 8 percent during this time, but they were still getting a comfortable chunk of a fast-expanding economy.

In the mid-1970s, the United States was confronted with an economic crisis called "stagflation," which meant rising prices and lowering demand for "consumer goods." In the United States and Europe, inflation rates went from about 3 percent in 1965 to about 12 percent in 1975.

There is serious debate about these economic changes. Most academics point to the high costs of the Vietnam War, which resulted in the first U.S. deficit of the twentieth century. This upset international investors, who dumped their dollars, lowering their value. Then, in 1971, in an effort to pay for the war, President Richard Nixon unpegged the dollar from the gold standard. Gold prices went up, the dollar went down, and inflation rates soared. Aggravating the trouble was the oil "crisis" in 1973, which drove up fuel prices and slowed economic production and growth even further.

Conservative scholars claimed the "stagflation crisis" was the result of high taxes on the rich and too much government regulation. This argument was especially attractive to the wealthy, who had seen their wealth dissipate in a serious way during this crisis. They responded by taking the opportunity to dismantle the programs of "embedded liberalism."

The crossover point from embedded liberalism into neoliberalism occurred with an event economists call the "Volker Shock." In 1979, Paul Volker, Chairman of the U.S. Federal Reserve, argued that the only way to stop inflation was to increase interest rates, which would make dollars more valuable. Interest rates rose to nearly 20 percent, and eventually inflation was controlled. Yet, it also resulted in high unemployment, higher rates of bankruptcies, and lower family income. This was not surprising; when corporations are forced to "cut costs," one of the first cost-cutting efforts is labor, and workers are laid off. Unemployment rates went up over 10 percent and most labor unions struggled to remain solvent and relevant. When President Richard Nixon lifted restrictions on capital flow, large corporations began locating facilities in countries with cheaper labor and less regulation, contributing to more unemployment.

The second blow to embedded liberalism was what President Ronald Reagan called "supply side" economics. This newly packaged old idea was a crucial component of neoliberalism. The idea was to cut tax rates to the rich, who would then invest the money in new production facilities, creating jobs and new business opportunities. Conservative economists called this policy the "trickle-down effect."

Reagan cut taxes to the rich from 70 percent to 28 percent, and reduced the maximum capital gains tax to 20 percent, the lowest since the Great Depression. Next, the Reagan Administration introduced another crucial component of neoliberalism—deregulation of banking and business activities. This phase of the neoliberal program was orchestrated by Alan Greenspan, who replaced Volker as Fed Chairman. Deregulation, it was argued, would "free" entrepreneurs and corporations from government constraints, resulting in more "open markets" and more creative financial opportunities.

The results of these policies created a huge windfall of wealth to the already rich, but not much "trickled down" to working people. For example, in 1973 the average real wage in the United States was $15.73 per hour; in 2000 it was $14.15 per hour. Over the same time, salaries of CEOs increased by an average of 400 percent. If anything, economic gain moved *upwards*, and not at a "trickle," but more like a torrent.

The current situation is similar; since 2000 the rich have gotten richer while working people have remained at the same level, or even fallen to lower levels of income and overall assets.

According to a report by Payscale, a compensation research company, average real wages have declined during the last seven years, while corporate profits soared—in 2015 corporate profits were up nearly 20 percent. In fact, for the first time in U.S. history, corporate earnings make up the largest share of GDP.

After 12 years of Republican administrations and Greenspan's continuous deregulation (into the Clinton Administration), the ideas of neoliberalism took hold firmly, not only in the financial sector, but also in the culture generally, especially in education. Besides intense corporate involvement in colleges and universities, corporations also invaded high schools and grade schools, which often accept corporate donations in return for certain conditions—such as fast food in the cafeteria, or the strategic placement of corporate names and logos.

As we noted earlier, most humans are dependent on corporations for their employment and survival. In the United States, neoliberalism spawned a "corporate culture" financed by the wealthy and disseminated through a network of "think tanks," institutions, schools, universities, and mainstream media outlets. The new mantra was that corporations don't need people—people need corporations. The assumption was that there are now corporations so big and powerful they ostensibly cannot be allowed to fail, even though the directors may make greedy or stupid decisions. The argument is that too many people will lose their jobs, and it would blow a hole in the economy and Wall Street. The U.S. government was "forced" to bail out several large investment banks and mortgage companies with billions of taxpayers' dollars, while, at the same time, it debated whether or not to cut food stamps to low income families. This process demonstrates that the focus of government efforts was on the corporate sector, rather than social relief programs.

Neoliberalism and the corporatization of nearly every facet of life—primarily via political power and money—have eroded the democratic process. With public spaces shrinking and private control of society increasing, there is less chance for social discourse and political engagement. Most citizens are passive onlookers to the mainstream political system, and participate actively only a few hours every few years. Even then, the political process is "sold" to citizens through the media, just as all other commodities (McDonald-Gibson, 2016).

Greenspan's deregulation program led partly to "creative" financial practices such as "derivatives" and "mortgage bundles," and led to the recession of 2007, which took full force in 2008 when millions lost their homes and jobs. At this time, millions still face foreclosure. Unemployment remains constant, and far too many of the "jobs recovered" involve part-time jobs for which employees are paid minimum wage and are not usually eligible for benefits. The income gap between rich and poor is the widest it's been since the 1920s.

Given such extraordinary conditions, how is it possible U.S. politicians are allowed to continue implementing neoliberal programs? We discovered several reasons: First, labor unions have been nearly wiped out and command little power or influence. Second, a large part of U.S. manufacturing has relocated overseas, and the labor market is changing rapidly into a tech-based service economy, which is less labor intensive. Third, with unemployment high and a stagnant manufacturing sector, there is an over-supply of workers, leading to low wage rates and an increase in "part-time" employees. Fourth, unlike the average citizen, corporations and their owners are heavily involved in the political system, not only providing generous donations to candidates and political parties, but also funding lobbyists, institutes, associations, and "think tanks" to directly influence congressional thinking. Fifth, through the hegemonic process, citizens are taught to believe and expect neoliberal principles and conditions—even though very few have ever heard the word "neoliberalism." Sixth, neoliberal programs convert citizens into consumers by equating "individual liberties" with "market freedoms." Seventh, and most important, U.S. citizens, as *consumers*, have been taught to focus on personal satisfaction rather than social and political responsibility.

We want to highlight the role of institutes, foundations, and industry associations in "selling" neoliberal policies to the public and to lawmakers. In the last 40 years a gigantic network of enterprises has been created, dedicated to everything from climate change to diaper disposal. Most of these enterprises are founded and funded by private interests—corporations, industry associations, or wealthy individuals. They fund "scientific study and research," lobby congress, and disseminate their "findings" through the popular media.

These are usually non-profit enterprises or foundations dedicated to particular segments of society—those in accordance with the wishes of the founders and funders. Now, it's no secret that most of the funding to the Heartland Institute is from oil corporations or wealthy individuals with oil holdings. Its pseudoscience and economics of climate change support the view that "global warming is not a crisis and that immediate action to reduce emissions is not necessary" (www. heartland.org, p. 19). The Institute's website announces its latest "conference" on climate change: "The conference's theme will be Climate Change: Scientific Debate and Economic Analysis. The theme reflects the fact that the scientific debate is not over and that economic analysis is more important than ever, now that legislation is being seriously considered."

Heartland gives a list of speakers and their organizational affiliations, the names of which are lofty and innocuous: Americans for Prosperity, American Enterprise Institute, International Center for a Scientific Ecology, Citizens for a Sound Economy, Competitive Enterprise Institute, Center for the Study of Public Choice, Science and Environmental Policy Project, New Hope Environmental Services, Center for the Study of Carbon Dioxide and Global Change, and Heritage Foundation. These are only a few of the hundreds of organizations that advance the programs of private interests under the guise of performing "public education and service." Most of these organizations are lavishly funded and employ scientists, professors, and former government officials.

Heartland has continued the fight against "alarmist" messages about global warming. A press release by Heartland announced the results of its "new study" demonstrating that global warming will actually be *beneficial*:

> The authors contend the world's economies are heavily dependent on fossil fuels because such fuels are and will continue to be safer, less expensive, more reliable, and of vastly greater supply than alternative fuels such as wind and solar. Dramatically reducing the use of fossil fuels would have devastating effects on workers and consumers of both the developed and developing worlds, leading to severe hardship and even deaths.

> Rather than continue to fight what is most likely a natural and unstoppable phenomenon, the authors call for adopting new energy and environmental policies that acknowledge current market and environmental realities. Such policies would encourage economic growth as the foundation for a cleaner environment, responsible development and use of fossil fuels until superior energy sources are found, and repeal of many of the regulations, subsidies, and taxes passed at the height of the man-made global warming scare. (2014:2)

The report stresses that global warming and increased carbon dioxide will have a beneficial effect on plant growth, with bigger, healthier plants, more production, and more profits. Plus, the warmer temperatures will offer a longer growing season and open up new areas of the Earth to agriculture.

Already there is a rising chorus of criticism in the wake of this announcement, claiming, among other things, that the focus is too narrow and not necessarily true. Also, it ignores the devastating effects of weather instability (Sachs, 2015; Idso, Singer, and Carter, 2014).

However, the point we make is that these organizations have the power to influence public debate and government policy. Spokespeople from these organizations are often featured in the mainstream media. Also, Heartland used its considerable funds to support a lawsuit against the state of Virginia to stop the state from enacting global warming legislation.

Very often these organizations have much better funding and better access than grass-roots programs, which are typically concentrated in the middle and lower portions of the economy. In this process corporations and wealthy individuals can pursue their private interests without getting directly involved publicly.

Once neoliberal policies were firmly established in the United States and Europe, they were exported to the rest of the world. Again, the occasion was the "Volker Shock." During the 1970s, U.S. investment banks flush with cash because of a stagnated domestic economy, made high-interest loans to foreign governments struggling to pay the high costs of rising fuel prices. It was believed this would be a safe investment, since it seemed unlikely a country could default.

These loans were in U.S. dollars and pegged to U.S. interest rates, and when the "Volker Shock" hit in the early eighties, interest rates climbed. The first country to edge close to default was Mexico, then others, and this subsequently touched off what is now known as the "third world debt crisis"—sovereign nations owing billions of dollars to private banks.

The International Monetary Fund (IMF) had been created to help countries through difficult times, using its own
money to make short-term loans. Now, however, the debts
were much too large for the IMF to service. Even scarier, at
least for Wall Street investors, were the very real prospects of
large-scale default and the crash of their banks. Eventually, the
Reagan Administration stepped in and used the IMF to make
sure these countries could pay their debts. The IMF offered to
roll over these debts at favorable interest rates providing these
countries agreed to "structural adjustment programs." Faced
with default, bad credit ratings, shrinking investment, and social unrest, these countries—mostly in Latin America—acted
as if they had little choice.

These "structural adjustment programs" followed neoliberal principles; a demand for government deregulation and
cutting subsidies to food, transportation, healthcare, and priva-
tizing public utilities, such as water and electricity. Further,
trade barriers should be lowered to provide a "level playing
field" for capital investment, where giant multinational corporations can expect to stomp anyone who shows up on the field.

The effects of these "structural adjustments" have been
harmful to most debtor nations—in some cases disastrous.
Their domestic sector, small and shaky in most cases, typically
cannot compete with big multinational corporations, particularly in the all-important agricultural sector. U.S. agribusiness
corporations produce huge amounts at low costs; further, they
benefit from generous subsidies from the government. They
can easily price their products below foreign producers, which
decreases their income and leads to unemployment. In Argentina, the grain producing sector collapsed; in Mexico the corn
producers suffered.

Neoliberal policies were further advanced with a series of
"free trade agreements" between the United States and other
countries, particularly in Latin America. Essentially, these

agreements are an alliance between the U.S. economic elite and the economic elite of the target country. Ostensibly, these "free trade agreements" are supposed to increase trade and investment, create jobs, and improve the social and economic well-being of all citizens. At least, this is how these agreements are "sold" to the public.

Again, we'll refer to Costa Rica as an example since it has a fairly stable social democracy, with the most sensitive sectors of the economy still in the hands of government monopolies—such as electricity, telecommunications, fuel, and gas. The government leaders of the United States and Costa Rica had reached a "fair trade" agreement, but the Costa Rican parliament could not muster the votes to ratify the agreement. The Costa Rican government called a national referendum on the issue.

The formal written agreement was over one thousand pages long and filled with legal and technical language. According to La Nación, the country's leading newspaper, fewer than five hundred Costa Ricans read the entire document, and most never read one word.

The "Yes" or "No" campaign on the referendum resembled a political campaign or product promotion. The "Yes" people and the "No" people presented 10 or 20 second commercials in the media, both sides using conventional commercial methods—grabby music, soft baritone voice-overs, attractive people, and lovely sound bites, such as "more jobs for everyone" and "a better life, a better future," or "loss of sovereignty" and "higher prices."

The "Yes" promotion was orchestrated by the wealthy class, including President Oscar Aries (patron of one of Costa Rica's wealthiest families and winner of the Nobel Peace Prize), who first proposed the agreement. Consequently, the "Yes" campaign had the most resources and saturated the media with happy, upbeat commercials. The "Yes" vote won, even though few of the citizens in Costa Rica knew exactly what they were voting about. Now multinational corporations and wealthy U.S. citizens invest heavily in Costa Rica, which boasts rich resources and a fairly stable social structure. Also, as happened with most other "free trade agreements," the Costa Rican agricultural sector is struggling to overcome the invasion of cheap food products from the United States. The cost of living keeps rising, and unemployment among Costa Rican young people is at record levels. Meanwhile, according to the terms of the agreement, the Costa Rican government has opened up the telecommunication industry to private investment and prepares to do the same with electricity and gas. Since the government subsidizes these industries, privatization will inevitably result in rising prices.

Wal-Mart, the biggest retailer in the world, bought most of Costa Rica's national grocery chains, but kept the names and logos the same. Most Costa Ricans are not aware there is no longer "competition" among these chains since they're owned by Wal-Mart. The profits go up north, into the pockets of shareholders. Costa Ricans work in these stores, but their wages are low (approximately three to four dollars an hour).

The North American Free Trade Agreement (NAFTA) is an economic alliance among Canada, the United States, and Mexico, initiated in 1994, under President Clinton. NAFTA was also crafted according to neoliberal policies—government deregulation and free access for investment and markets. Mexico, as the weakest economy in this consortium, felt the impact most solidly. Giant multinational corporations immediately flooded Mexico with "consumer goods" and turned the manufacturing sector into assembly plants of U.S. products for export.

From 1980 to 2010, Mexico's per capita GDP rose by 22 percent, but this is less than the average of all Latin American countries—33 percent—and considerably less than the 66 percent rise in GDP in the United States during this same period. Apart from this modest long-term rise in per capita GDP, the number of Mexican citizens living below the poverty line has not changed significantly in recent decades; in 1984 it was 53 percent, in 2010 it was 51 percent. However, Mexico was hit hard in the mid-1990s by an economic "crisis," and the poverty rate soared to nearly 70 percent. Although the poverty rate has improved since then, it is still a severe problem; over 50 million people live in poverty. However, as in other countries in the western hemisphere, wealthy Mexicans increased their wealth considerably during this time.

Meanwhile, Mexican citizens feel the impact of these conditions and they are not content; according to Consulta Mitofsky, a Mexican survey research group, in 2014 eighty percent of Mexicans said the economic situation in their country was getting worse, up from 60 percent in 2006 and 57 percent who said the same in 2001.

"Structural adjustment programs" and free trade agreements among governments advance neoliberal policies on the formal, legal level. And, neoliberal ideals are also propagated through a hegemonic process of cultural dissemination, particularly from the United States.

U.S. movies, music, television programs, video games, fads, and fashions have flooded most cultures in the world, and the main underlying message is *consumerism*. However, they also carry messages encouraging particular connotations of sexism and racism, since these attitudes also permeate the Cultural Model. These U.S. programs are dubbed in the appropriate languages for foreign audiences, and the dialogue and images convey powerful messages. Furthermore, the commercials that accompany these programs usually are dominated by promotions for U.S. products.

These cultural transfers can have important consequences. For example, the U.S. fast-food industry invaded countries around the world with franchises and television commercials.

In the case of Costa Rica, the U.S. fast-food industry moved in quickly, accompanied by intense promotions, mainly through television. After almost 30 years of exposure to these cultural elements, Costa Rican health officials have announced an obesity epidemic (similar to that in the U.S.), which has nearly overwhelmed the public health system. They attribute the epidemic to a shift from a traditional diet of rice and beans to a diet of hamburgers, pizzas, fried chicken, tacos, and donuts.

From our perspective, it would appear that neoliberal leaders are intent on spreading the ideals of neoliberalism and consumerism to all the peoples of the world through "free trade programs" and the hegemonic process. The spread of neoliberalism is not only deep but wide. Its scope runs far beyond the image of the Western societies. Dubai and Beijing are only the tip of the proverbial iceberg or in this case the more obvious cutting-edge of the neoliberal thrust. For a heuristic related process, compare NAFTA with BREXIT, for example, which is only the latest development in the conflicted relationship between the UK and the EU that has played out over the past 50 years. There is a giant contradiction brewing within these efforts: With wealth continuing to concentrate in the hands of the wealthy, there will not be enough people who can afford to buy "consumer goods." This change might precipitate the collapse of the entire system, which makes no sense in our view. In addition, much of this "wealth" is represented in speculative assets that exist as numbers in accounting books, rather than tangible resources. Therefore, a great segment of this "wealth" consists of nothing more than hopes and daydreams, and is highly vulnerable to sudden changes in *mood*. It's not uncommon to see the "market" swing wildly from day to day, usually based on "fears" or "optimism."

We encountered a dialogue between an indigenous person and a college professor that illustrates the problematic quality of the neoliberal philosophy:

A college professor stood on the bank of a river and watched as an Indian paddled his small boat up to the dock. Inside the boat were several large fish. The professor complimented the Indian on the quality of his fish and asked him how long it took to catch them.

The Indian replied, "Only a little while."

The professor then asked, "Why don't you stay out longer and catch more fish?"

The Indian answered, "Why should I do that? I catch enough to feed my family."

"What do you do with the rest of your time?" The professor asked.

The Indian replied, "I sleep late, play with my children, take a nap with my wife, then stroll into the village where I sip wine and play music with my friends. I have a full and busy life."

The professor shook his head with a skeptical expression. "I am a Stanford business professor and I can give you good advice. You should spend more time fishing, catch more fish, sell the fish, and buy a bigger boat. With a bigger boat you'll catch even more fish, and you can buy more boats. Eventually you'll have a fleet of fishing boats. Then, instead of selling your fish to a middleman, you can open your own cannery. You'll make a lot of money. You could leave this small fishing village and move to a big city where you can expand your business."

The Indian thought about that for a moment, and then asked, "How much time will all this take?"

The Stanford business professor answered, "15 or 20 years."

"And then what will I do?" asked the Indian.

The professor laughed. "That's the best part. When the time is right you would announce an IPO, sell your company stock to the public and become very rich. You could make millions."

"Millions? Then what?"

"Then you can retire and move to a small village where you could sleep late, play with your kids, take naps with your spouse, and stroll to the village where you can sip wine and play music with your friends."

This story illustrates the irony and danger of neoliberalism. Yet, most humans cannot see the danger because the ideas of continuous consumption and wealth accumulation are prominent fixtures of the Cultural Model—they also appear to be a facade of *reality*.

CROSSROADS

Earth has entered a dangerous phase in its existence, a crucial crossroads, where political machinations and history might condense into a point of no return. Given the fragile condition of Earth's atmosphere and the increase in human consumption and conflict, the situation seems ominous. Yet, we recall that the nuclear attacks at the end of World War II in 1945 have not been repeated, even though many more nuclear weapons have been deployed by more countries. This is a strange fact, but not so mysterious—there is a deep-seated horror inside most human hearts toward nuclear weapons.

Although nuclear weapons have not been used since 1945, nuclear power and nuclear weapons have become popular again, at least among the "superpowers." Russia and China continue to build new atomic weapons and improve old ones; India and Pakistan have built nuclear arsenals; England and France have sizable nuclear weapons stockpiles; Israel is widely assumed to possess around 200 nuclear warheads of various sizes; North Korea apparently developed a nuclear capability; some countries believe Iran hopes to build an atomic bomb. In June 2016, U.S. President Obama announced a trillion dollar program to "up-grade" and "improve" U.S. nuclear forces.

This reliance on "nuclear deterrence" may actually increase the possibility of annihilation. For example, the U.S. has never rejected the option of "first use" of nuclear weapons (even though nuclear weapons have been "used" twice already). The U.S. relies on a "counter-force" strategy, which means their warheads are targeted on Chinese and Russian ICBMs and missile submarines. Therefore, the U.S. can shoot first, before those opposing missiles leave their silos.

However, aside from a deliberate use of nuclear weapons, we have uncovered several incidents of accidents and misunderstandings that led to the highest levels of "launch status." Here again, the enormous destructive power of these weapons—capable of obliterating entire countries—requires a hyper vigilance of one's nuclear-armed "enemies." This vigilance is almost completely dependent on highly sophisticated technology, which is prone to breakdowns or "false information," and could lead to a desperate or panicky response. We have found several cases when machine errors triggered a higher alert status.

The possibility of a nuclear exchange increases during times of great flux and tension, as nuclear-armed "superpowers" maneuver boldly against each other in a deadly political game of hegemony and access to resources. As a backdrop to this nuclear menace, the level and degree of human consumption is increasing, continually interfering with the planet's ecosystem and prompting high rates of extinction. All these events crowd together into a tight ball of international tensions and threats.

Since part of our responsibility in this sector of the galaxy is to protect all planets and life-forms, we are sending this report with the following overview: Not all the news is bad. Exceptional humans have gained political and social prominence by working to protect the Earth and its people. Agness Gonxha Bojaxhiu (aka Mother Teresa), Mahatma Gandhi, Jane Goodall, Martin Luther King, Jr., Vine Deloria, Jr., Nelson Mandela, and Tewolde Egziabher are only a few examples of protectors of Mother Earth. As Mother Teresa once noted, "If you judge people, you have no time to love them."

Also, there are numerous important social movements fighting for significant change. The social and political revolutions among various Arab countries, initially called ("Arab Spring"), continue and are spreading around the globe to other, non-Arab countries. Importantly, the revolutions among Arab countries demonstrated how communications technology can not only confer power on the elite, but also give power to the people. In Tunisia, Libya, and Egypt, cell phones and the internet played a significant role in uniting and organizing the opposition. Although some of these governments still try to impede or block these communications, often such information moves within these countries. Moreover, images and videos of revolutionary activities were uploaded to the internet and impacted world opinion and related social movements.

The movement called *Occupy Wall Street* appears to have spawned critical thinking and resistance that is impacting more recent movements (White, 2016). The uproar over the leaking of government and private information — exposed by Edward Snowden, Bradley Manning, and Julian Assange, among others—is growing and tests the notion of national security rather than global security (Gellman, 2016).

We want to warn the humans: Beware of the fixed "social reality," for it is false. Our universe is not "fixed"; the entire natural mystic is in constant dynamic flux and movement. Peter Berger (2011:19) notes that a particular frame of reference searches for levels of reality beyond so-called official interpretations of society—or even the "social reality" we take for granted. The goal is to "see through" the facades of "social reality" to find out "what is really going on underneath it all."

Social reality reflects elements of constant change. Although any present Cultural Model appears as solid as "reality," it is a social construct and subject to change. Crucial changes for the Earth will necessitate a new Cultural Model. The current Model, centered on consumerism, appears to lead to chaos, war, and doom. The majority of humans spend most of their waking hours engaged in "work" so they may consume—and not merely to survive, but also to purchase "consumer goods" that contribute to the basis of ranking, status, and social conflict. An alternative Cultural Model, centered on Nature, is paramount in saving the Earth and its ecosphere and all life-forms, including the humans.

Although our report tends to focus on conflict, danger, and absurdity, these are observations of human behavior on Earth in the aggregate—from a global perspective. However, we want to stress that most individual humans display virtuous qualities. Social relations within most cultures are guided by consensual regard, where the millions of daily interactions among citizens and neighbors are performed in an atmosphere of peace and courtesy. Much of the conflict, danger, and absurdity seem to emanate from the machinations of political and corporate power.

We might examine more closely the quote by Vine Deloria (1973) that we mentioned in our introduction: "If all things are related, the unity of creation demands that each life form contribute its intended contribution. Any violation of another entity's right to existence in and of itself is a violation of the nature of creation and a degradation of religious reality itself" (p. 99).

And, as the wise Ishmael said: "Takers accumulate knowledge about what works well for things. Leavers accumulate knowledge about what works well for people" (Quinn 1992:119).

The humans can save themselves and their primal Mother if they change their global culture. Although we are aliens and friends, we're not angels or magicians. Also, we know that those who try to help, such as missionaries, can sometimes make things worse. We observe and report as accurately as possible, and if the humans save themselves and their planet, we will rejoice with all living things.

REFERENCES

Introduction:

Berger, Peter L. 2011. *Invitation to Sociology: A Humanistic Perspective*. New York: Open Road Media.

Frank, Andre Gunder, and Denemark, Robert. 2015. *Reorienting the 19th Century: Global Economy in the Continuing Asian Age*. New York: Routledge Press.

Lauderdale, Pat, ed. 2011. *A Political Analysis of Deviance*. Whitby, Canada: de Sitter Publications.

Leonard, Dick and Robert Taylor. 2016. *The Routledge Guide to the European Union*. London: Routledge.

McPherson, Guy. 2013. *Going Dark*. Baltimore, MD: Publish America.

Oliverio, Annamarie. 1998. *The State of Terror*. Albany, NY: State University of New York Press.

Sachs, Jeffrey. 2015. *The Age of Sustainable Development*. New York: Columbia University Press.

The Japan Times "China hands Russia get of jail free card: $400 billion gas deal." May 24, 2014. Retrieved June 15, 2014 (http://www.japantimes.co.jp/news/2014/05/22/world/china-hands-russia-get-jail-free-card-400-billion-gas-deal/#.U9VyD7FnBLY).

Consumerism:

Cohen, Lizabeth. 2003. *A Consumers' Republic: The Politics of Mass Consumption in Postwar America*. New York: Random House.

Cruit, Michael. 2014. *Fastball Fari.* Orange, NJ: Summer Game Books.

Deloria, Vine Deloria Jr. 1973. *God is Red: A Native View of Religion.* New York: Putnam Publishing Group.

Heilbroner, Robert. 1999. *The Worldly Philosophers: The Lives, Times and Ideas of the Great Economic Thinkers*, 7th Edition. New York: Touchstone.

Mander, Jerry. 1978. *Four Arguments for the Elimination of Television.* New York: Harper Collins.

Martineau, Pierre. 1958. "Social Classes and Spending Behavior," *Journal of Marketing* 23(2):55-68.

Mayer, Jane. 2016. *Dark Money: The Hidden History of the Billionaires behind the Rise of the Radical Right.* New York: Doubleday.

Mies, Maria. 1986. *Patriarchy and Accumulation on a World Scale.* London: Zed Books.

Nader, Laura. 2002. *The Life of Law.* Berkeley: University of California Press.

Profita, Cassandra. 2013. "Recyclers Limit Plastic Collection as China Stops Buying." Oregon Public Broadcasting. May 2. Retrieved June 15, 2014 (http://www.networkedblogs.com/L8j6W).

Proctor, Robert. 2008. "Agnotology: A Missing Term to Describe the Cultural Production of Ignorance (and Its Study)." Pp. 312-339 in *Agnotology: The Making & Unmaking of Ignorance*, edited by Robert N. Proctor and Londa Schiebinger. Stanford: Stanford University Press.

Shabazz, Rashad. 2015. Spatializing Blackness. Champaign: University of Illinois Press.

Quinn, Daniel. 1992. *Ishmael: An Adventure of the Mind and Spirit*. New York: Random House.

Education:

Adamson, Frank, Björn Åstrand, and Linda Darling-Hammond. 2016. *Global Education Reform: How Privatization and Public Investment Influence Education Outcomes*. New York: Routledge

Bennett, William J. and David Wilezol. 2013. *Is College Worth It?: A Former United States Secretary of Education and a Liberal Arts Graduate Expose the Broken Promise of Higher Education* Nashville, TN: Thomas Nelson.

Berger, Peter L. 2011. *Invitation to Sociology: A Humanistic Perspective*. New York: Open Road Media.

Gouldner, Alvin. 1970. *The Coming Crisis of Western Sociology*. New York: Basic Books.

Institute for College Access and Success. 2014. Retrieved August 4, 2014 (http://www.ticas.org/).

Mayer, Jane. 2016. *Dark Money: The Hidden History of the Billionaires Behind the Rise of the Radical Right*. New York: Doubleday.

Schaeffer, Robert. 2016. *Understanding Globalization*. New York: Rowman & Littlefield.

Teachout, Zephyr. 2016. *Corruption in America: From Benjamin Franklin's Snuff Box to Citizens United*. Boston: Harvard University Press.

Drugs:

Centers for Disease Control and Prevention, *National Health Interview*

Survey, 2012:63. Atlanta GA: Centers for Disease Control and Prevention.

Chiarello, Elizabeth. 2015. "The War on Drugs Comes to the Pharmacy Counter: Frontline Work in the Shadow of Discrepant Institutional Logics," *Law & Social Inquiry* 40:1, 86-122.

Conners, Keith. 2013. "The Selling of Attention Deficit Disorder." *The New York Times*, Dec. 14. Retrieved June 1, 2014 (http://www.nytimes.com/2013/12/15/health/the-selling-of-attention-deficit-disorder.html?pagewanted=all&_r=0).

O'Brien, Dan. 2002. *Buffalo for the Broken Heart: Restoring Life to a Black Hills Ranch*. New York: Random House.

National Institute on Drug Abuse, (www.drugabuse.gov p. 60). Retrieved August 5, 2014

War:

Bacevich, Andrew. 2015. *America's War for the Greater Middle East: A Military History*. New York: Random House.

Bergen, Peter. 2016. *United States of Jihad: Investigating America's Homegrown Terrorists*. New York: Crown.

Eisenhower, Dwight D. 1961. Farewell Address, Jan. 17. Retrieved from (http://www.ourdocuments.gov/doc.php?flash=true&doc=90).

Morris, Ian. 2014. *War! What Is It Good For?: Conflict and the Progress of Civilization from Primates to Robots*. New York: Farrar, Straus and Giroux.

The Medical Consequences of Thermonuclear War. 1962. *New England Journal of Medicine* 266(22):1126-1155. Retrieved June 1, 2014 (http://www.nejm.org/toc/nejm/266/22).

Neoliberalism:

Bretton Woods Conference. 1944. Retrieved August 5, 2014 http://fraser.stlouisfed.org/specialcollection-document/?id=4701.

Heartland Institute. 2014. "Benefits of Global Warming Greatly Exceed Costs, New Study Says." March 24. Retrieved June 14, 2014 (http://heartland.org/press-releases/2014/03/24/benefits-global-warming-greatly-exceed-costs-new-study-says).

Idso, Craig, S. Fred Singer, Robert M. Carter. 2014. *Climate Change Reconsidered II: Biological Impacts.* Center for the Study of Carbon Dioxide and Global Change; Science and Environmental Policy Project; Heartland Institute. Retrieved June 1, 2014 (http://heartland.org/policy-documents/climate-change-reconsidered-ii-biological-impacts).

McDonald-Gibson, Charlotte. 2016. *Cast Away.* New York: The New Press.

Crossroads:

Gellman, Barton. 2016. *Dark Mirror: Edward Snowden and the American Surveillance State.* New York: Penguin Press.

White, Micah. 2016. *The End of Protest.* Toronto: Knopf Canada

AFTERWORD

We would like to thank Annmarie Oliverio, Dillion Diffie, William Quetone, and Steve McLaughlin for their comments for revisions on earlier drafts of this work. Kath Wilham provided meticulous editorial support, and she exceeded our expectations with crucial substantive suggestions. We also appreciate the reactions from the students at Arizona State University, and support from Barrett, The Honors College, which led to the some of the ideas in this book. The Herbert Blumer Institute on the Boca Rio Sierpe and the Social Research Institute of Arizona provided essential support for our work. We hope that this new edition will be useful in the pursuit of justice rather than just us.

Michael Cruit and Pat Lauderdale

Index

embedded liberalism, 123, 124
environmental and social disaster, 24

F

free trade agreements, 131, 133, 134

G

global ecosystem, 25, 28
globalogy, 4
global warming, 26, 27, 35, 36, 121, 128, 130
GMO foods, 67, 68
Gouldner, Alvin, 69
Gramsci, Antonio, 3
Great Pacific Garbage Patch, 32, 34

H

Heartland Institute, 128, 130
hegemonic process, 5, 40, 127, 134
Hellfire missile, 108, 112, 114
higher education, 61, 62, 66
Ho Chi Minh, 105
homogenizing the culture, 22
human population, 28, 29, 37, 93

I

illegal drug use, 77
income gap, 45, 127
indigenous world view, 25
Ishmael, 28

K

Kaufman, Beatrice, 14
Keynes, John Maynard, 122
Khomeinim, Ayatollah, 100
Kissinger, Henry, 104

L

landfills, 31, 32, 34, 37

M

Mander, Jerry, 23
manipulate, 20
manufacturing consent, 50
market segmentation, 9, 10, 44
Martineau, Pierre, 10

mass marketing, 7, 17, 95
media industry, 21
Monsanto, 66
moral entrepreneurs, 115

N

Nader, Laura, 44
NAFTA, 133, 135
National Security Agency (NSA), 110, 111, 112, 113
neoliberalism, 122, 124, 137
Noriega, Manuel, 103
nuclear warheads, 97, 108, 121, 138
nuclear weapons, 1, 56, 96, 115, 138

O

Occupy Wall Street, 140
Oliverio, Annamarie, 3
opium, 74, 75, 77, 82, 89
overdose, 82

P

patriotism, 55
plastic, 31, 32, 80
political deviance, 110
political deviants, 6, 54, 60, 115, 119
political power, 4, 5, 35, 57, 91, 102, 118, 126
poverty line, 38, 134

Q

Quinn, Daniel, 28

R

Reza Shah Pahlavi, Mohammad, 99
Roosevelt, Kermit, 99

S

Schwarzkopf, H. Norman, 99
Smith, Adam, 8
sociology, 2, 69, 71
supply side economics, 125

W

Wilezol, David, 62

Made in the USA
Las Vegas, NV
21 July 2021

26793060R00094